A STUDENT'S GUIDE TO THE INTERNET

A STUDENT'S GUIDE TO THE INTERNET

Surfing for Success in Economics

1998-1999

Scott Simkins
North Carolina Agricultural Technical State University

Jim Barbour
Elon College

Contributors:
Marian B. Wood
Raymond D. Frost,
Central Connecticut State University
Judy Strauss,
Central Connecticut State University
Andrew T. Stull

Prentice Hall
Upper Saddle River, NJ 07458

Development: *Joan Waxman, Audrey Regan, and Steve Deitmer*
Interior design and formatting: *Theresa Festa*
Cover design: *Lorraine Castellano*
Advertising copy and design: *Eve Adams*
Production manager: *Richard Bretan*

Printed in the United States of America

10 9 8 7 6 5 4 3 2 1

ISBN 0-13-081523-3

What's Inside

Preface

The Internet is growing fast. We are in the middle of a story with an unpredictable outcome. Businesses and individuals are jumping on the electronic-communications bandwagon at an incredible rate. Still, some critics call the Net a fad. It's been some time since we've had something this exciting to debate!

We believe that the Internet will prove to be an extremely useful tool for your education and for business planning and operations across the globe. The Internet search capabilities and resource sites can aid any discipline by opening a high-speed gateway to a wealth of information. Also, the Net can assist with text-based communication: one-to-one e-mail conversation and e-mail conferencing via newsgroups and mailing lists, for example. Whether you're giving or receiving, the Internet can serve you well. And the more you know about how it works, the more the Internet can help you. We hope this guide answers your questions and gets you as excited about the Internet as we are.

We've set up our Internet guide this way:

Chapter 1 Frequently Asked Questions (FAQs)

Through its question-and-answer format, this chapter introduces you to the Internet and gives you a taste of where it comes from and what makes it tick.

Chapter 2 Up and Running: The Search is On

From basic searches to more advanced investigations, this chapter teaches you how to reach out across the Internet to find what you need.

Chapter 3 Getting Your Message Out in Style: E-Mail and Other Enhancements

Turn here to learn how to operate e-mail through your Internet connection. And do you need to know more about chat rooms, newsgroups, mailing lists? Do you want to customize your browser? This chapter will help you out.

Chapter 4 Sources of Economic Information on the Internet

Look over this in-depth presentation of how the Internet can help you gather the most important economic information.

Chapter 5 Turning Economic Information into Economic Knowledge

Take the information you've gathered from the Internet and turn it into the knowledge you need to analyze, forecast, and make economic decisions.

Chapter 6 Online Information About Careers, Graduate School, and Jobs

Filled with Internet addresses, this chapter tells you how to create an electronic resume and get started on finding that perfect job.

Chapter 7 Distance Learning

What do you look for in an online class? We take a look at distance learning in general, then follow a student taking a class over the Internet.

Appendix 1 Business-related Internet Addresses

This appendix organizes a wealth of Internet addresses by business discipline.

Appendix 2 Glossary

We give you what you need to speak the Internet language.

Chapter 1
Frequently Asked Questions (FAQs)

Many sites on the Internet use the Frequently Asked Questions (FAQ) format to help guide users and give them quick, useful answers to common questions. Often the FAQ page opens with a list of those questions that the people who built the page believe will be on many users' minds. Very often, these questions contain a hot button -- a hyperlink – to the answer. Users scan the list for a question they would like answered and then jump to the answer. We have kept our printed FAQ list especially small so that you can jump in and get started. Once you develop search skills from the early exercises in this book, you won't need us to answer your questions: You'll be able to search the Net yourself.

What is the Internet?

The Internet – often called simply "the Net" – is a network of computers reaching every country in the world. It is similar in some ways to the telephone system. Just as you can call people anywhere in the world, so too can you contact their computers as long as they are connected to the Net. But the Internet is more than computers and their contents: It is a social space where users communicate. It is this feature, as well as the fact that there is no governing body, that allows users to shape the Net. The Net is truly a grassroots development.

How did the Net develop?

The Internet has been around since the 1960s, when the Defense Department set it up as a fail-safe way of relaying messages in case of a nuclear attack. As a result the Internet is quite robust – communications almost always go through – though at times rather slowly. From the '60s until the early '90s the Internet's main users were the Defense Department and researchers in industry and education. These people plugged into the Net to share access to distant supercomputers and to send electronic mail. In those days, the Net was fairly hard to use and it was difficult to find your way around. Outside of a fairly small community, not that many people knew of, or cared much about, the Internet. All that changed in the mid-'90s.

Three major developments have revolutionized the way we use the Internet: the birth of the World Wide Web (WWW or Web), hyperlinks, and graphical browsers. Even though we use the terms "Internet" and "Web" interchangeably, the Web is a part of the Internet. It began as a standard that defined how to travel from computer to computer throughout the world by following embedded links in a screen display of written words (text). A click on the link and you were instantly transported to another computer as directed by the embedded instruction. Such clickable text was called hypertext. The Web and hypertext made it easy to get around because they formed a basis for navigation in Cyberspace. What was missing however were pictures, icons, and color. People like a graphical interface because it is intuitive and easy to master. The development of graphical browsers solved this problem.

Browsers are software programs that view information on the Internet. The most prominent browsers are Netscape Navigator (or Communicator) and Microsoft Internet Explorer. Graphical browsers allow users to click on images as well as text links to navigate in a multimedia world. Not only can sites contain text and graphics, but they can also contain sound, video, and even 3D video. Graphical browsers have brought visual appeal and entertainment value to the Web. The Web, hyperlinks, and graphical browsers have made Cyberspace a very friendly place and have driven the rush to get connected.

Just how popular is the Net today?

are connecting to the Net at a phenomenal rate, and the number of Web sites is doubling every 50 days. But this rush to the Net has created two problems.

First, the Internet is becoming slow. If 10 people use the same line, they each get one-tenth of the line's capacity (or bandwidth). If 100 people use the same line, then their share is cut to one-hundredth. Similarly, the computers with Web sites on the Internet – computers we call content providers – can be overworked by the increase in users. A computer that can handle 10 people simultaneously accessing its content may come to its knees when 100 people try accessing it at the same time. Popularity in Cyberspace comes with a price!

Second, the Net contains so much material that it has become difficult for users to find their way around. Fortunately, there are tools that help. These are known as search engines, and they find Net destinations for you. Knowing how to use search engines well is an essential survival skill in Cyberspace. Consequently, we'll take a look at this topic soon.

Where is the Internet?

The Internet is everywhere.

Because a person can get on the Internet through a standard phone line, the Internet is anywhere in the world that one can find a telephone. Once a user connects to an Internet computer, that computer serves as a gateway to the rest of the global network. Computers offering services on the Internet are scattered throughout the world. Fortunately, users do not need to know their geographic whereabouts while on the Net. All the user needs is the Internet address, also known as the URL (Universal Resource Locator), of the computer. A URL is similar to a postal address, providing all the information needed to locate a specific site on the Internet. Each URL has a few basic parts, just like a residential address. Internet addresses (URLs) may seem confusing at first, but think of them as nothing more than postal addresses squished together without any spaces. Let's dissect a URL to give you an idea of how an Internet address is constructed.

For example, the Internet address of the Martha and Spencer Love School of Business at Elon College (LSB) is:

http://www.elon.edu/lsb/index.html

Reading backward from the "forward slash" or "/" following ".edu" in the address above, we discover that it is an educational institution (*edu*) within the Elon College campus (*elon*), that it is the World Wide Web (*www*) server of the college, and that the files should be sent from the Elon College machine to yours using Hypertext Transfer Protocol (*http*). To the right of this first part of the address and reading forward, we find that the file in question is in the Love School of Business directory on the server (*lsb*) and that the file is named index and written in Hypertext Markup Language (*html*).

As it turns out, the default file that your browser will open is the one named index.html, so it is not necessary to include that in the address. Additionally the **http://** in front of the address is the default transfer protocol, so that is generally not included either. Thus the Web address will generally be presented as

www.elon.edu/lsb

Unlike postal addresses, most Internet addresses are not nearly so revealing as to location as the example above. It is not that the service is trying to conceal its location, but rather that on the Web the physical location of the information does not really matter. For example, does it matter to the user wanting to make an airline reservation where the Web site

www.travelocity.com

is located?

In this sense Web addresses are perhaps more similar to a telephone 800 number than a postal address. When dialing an 800 number the user doesn't usually know the location of a business. In the same way, Internet users do not always know the physical location of the information they are viewing. The information could be on a computer in the next room or across the world.

How is the Internet organized?

Net addresses carry one of several major Internet address classifications, known as top-level domain names. These appear as the last item in an address – for example, the ".edu" that appears in the Elon College school address and the ".com" in the travel services address we just presented. These domain names tell you the type of site you are connecting to. The following are important top-level domain names:

.com	**commercial**
.edu	**educational**
.gov	**government**
.net	**Internet service provider**
.org	**non-profit organization**

Knowing the domain names may help you as you search the Net. You can often guess a site address by using the organization name and domain name. For example, the site for Coca-Cola is www.coca-cola.com, and the site for Microsoft is www.microsoft.com.

Who is out there?

We have compared the Internet to the telephone system: a global communication network of computers. But who is sitting there, hunched over a keyboard, using these computers? Content providers, advertisers, and the audience.

Content Providers

First are the content providers. These are the businesses, universities, governments, and other organizations that allow others to peek into their computers. For example, North Carolina Agricultural and Technical State University maintains a computer called a Web server at its campus, on which information about the university, its programs, and its faculty, staff, and students is kept. The information on this computer is available 24 hours a day for anyone to view. Who created this information? Faculty, staff, and students at the University created Web "pages" to inform others about courses, athletic programs, and academic programs available at the university. In many cases, faculty members provide course notes, outlines, and even entire courses on the Web. Of course, these resources had to be created before they could be shared – that is the job of content providers. Anyone who has access to a Web server can provide information for others to see on the Web.

Advertisers

Second are advertisers. These are the corporations that pay content providers for space on their Web pages. For example, when you log on to a search engine's home page (search engines are the "telephone books" of the Internet), you generally will see announcements from advertisers who are paying for the space. This is how the search engines are able to offer their services for free. Topping the list is the Yahoo! search site with annual sales approaching $70 million. But even a small game site like Happy Puppy can earn $1.5 million a year selling ads. The top 50 advertisers spend over $180 million a year on ads. Leading the list is Microsoft, with expenditures of $30 million.

Audience

Finally, there is the audience. These are the people who travel the Web to find information from content providers that will be useful or entertaining. In addition to retrieving data from Web servers, the audience also uses the Internet to communicate to other people via e-mail, to post messages to newsgroups, and to just sit back and surf the Net for personal pleasure.

How do I connect to the Internet?

Users surf the Net from home, business, school, or the library, almost always for a fee. In businesses, schools, and libraries the organization often pays the charge and even provides the computers. That is the case in most universities, where access to the Internet is often provided in campus computer labs. You may be paying a "computer fee" to help support this service.

Internet Service Providers

Home users must provide their own computers and pay their own way. Every Internet connection goes through an Internet Service Provider (ISP). These organizations buy very high bandwidth connections to the Internet backbone and then resell it (many times over) in smaller pieces to subscribers. America Online, Microsoft Network, and AT&T are three examples of ISPs. To find an ISP you can visit the Netscape and Yahoo! sites (shown below) for a listing or consult your local telephone book's Yellow Pages.

http://home.netscape.com/assist/isp_select/
http://www.yahoo.com/Business_and_Economy/Companies/Internet_Services/Access_Providers/National__U_S__/

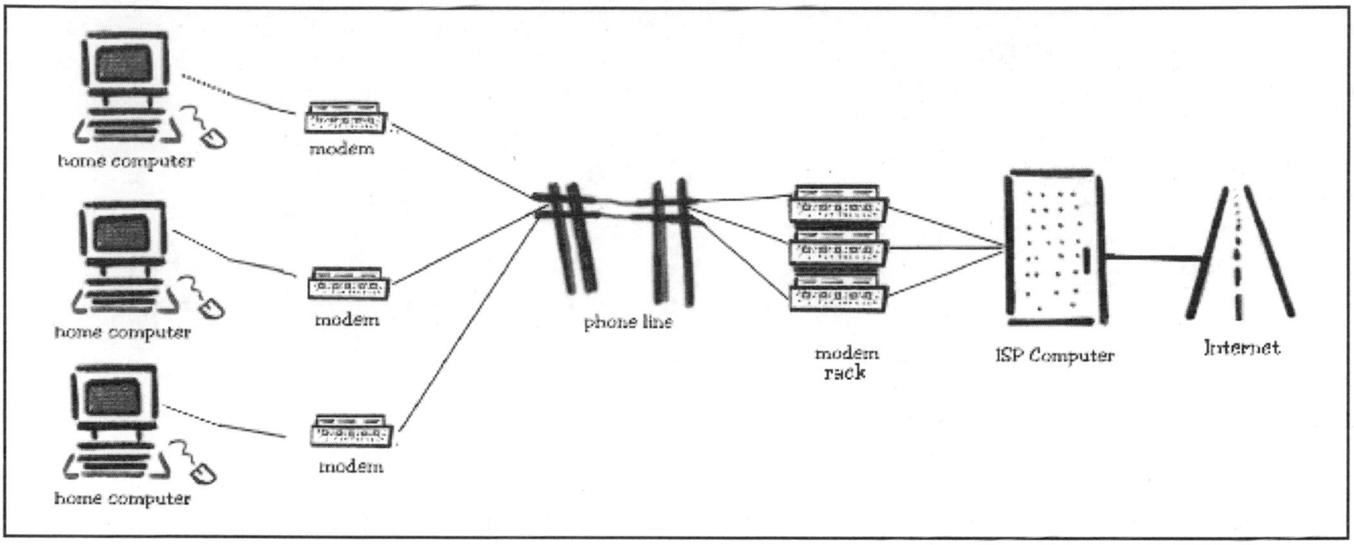

Figure 1.1 Your home computer connects to the Internet through an Internet Service Provider (ISP).

Modems

The connection from home to the ISP is typically over a phone line using a device called a modem. The modem translates the computer signals to sound waves, which are then decoded by a modem connected to a computer at the ISP receiving the call. Modems are an inexpensive means of getting connected, but they are somewhat slow.

A recent technological advance called X2 allows modems to receive information off the Internet at a rate of over 50,000 characters per second. And while 50,000 characters per second is faster than any of us can read, consider what it takes to handle graphics. A full-screen picture can easily exceed 1,000,000 characters (bytes), and video requires changing that picture 32 times per second. Fortunately, some clever techniques (called algorithms) compress graphics, sound, and video so that they can travel over the phone lines.

Recently, some cable companies have begun to offer high speed Internet service over cable TV wire using a device called a cable modem. The cable TV wire into your home has a much greater bandwidth than a telephone line and allows for high quality video. The marketplace will determine whether this becomes a viable option.

Communication Software and Web Browsers

Home users need communication software and a Web browser to connect to the Web and access the information there. The software controls the modem and maintains a connection with the ISP. Web browsers such as Netscape's Navigator and Microsoft's Internet Explorer are graphical user interfaces that operate over the established network connection. No matter what kind of connection you have to the Internet you will need to purchase or download a Web browser to view information on the Web. Netscape Navigator and Microsoft Internet Explorer, the two most popular Web browsers, are both freely available on the Web.

High Speed Connections

Organizations, like universities, schools, and corporations typically have a higher speed line (greater bandwidth) into the Internet. Those of you who connect to the Internet through one of these connections will find it is much faster than a modem. However, since the high speed line is shared, as the number of users in the organization increases, the speed with which each communicates decreases accordingly.

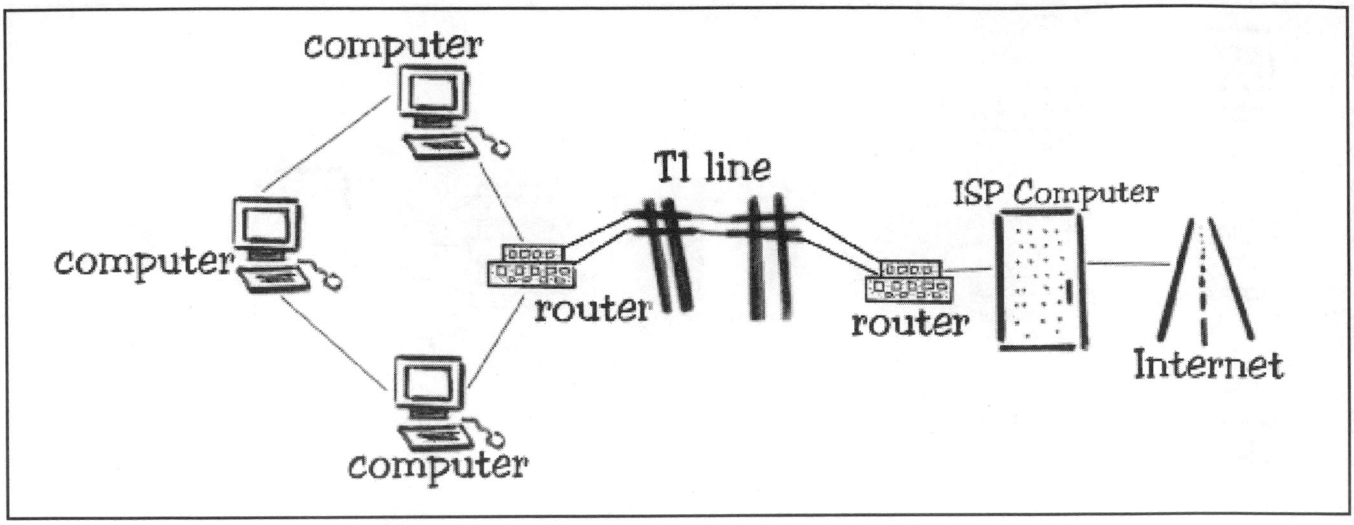

Figure 1.2 In many businesses, signals from individual computers travel through a T1 line on their way to the Internet.

The business communications channel typically consists of a leased digital line (a T1 or fractional T1 line) connected to the ISP. The T1 line connects to one computer on the Local Area Network (LAN) called the router. The router is able to direct signals to and from all computers on the network to the ISP along the T1 line. In this manner all users achieve an Internet connection by sharing a single line. You will probably never see the router or T1 line since they are typically locked away in a wiring closet. The following table summarizes this information.

Component	From Home	From an Organization
Communications Channel	Regular telephone line	Fractional T1 line connected to a Frame Relay Network
Communications Hardware	Modem with X2 technology	Local Area Network (LAN) and a router
Communications Software	Dialer; Web browser	LAN operating system and a Web browser
Computer (recommended specs-you can get by with less)	200 MHz Pentium II 32 MB RAM 2 GB Hard drive Sound card Speakers	Same

Questions to Ask Before Selecting an ISP

For home use, most ISP's charge monthly flat rate billing with unlimited access. The charge now averages about $20 per month for unlimited usage, although recently prices have started rising. Shop around for the best price and the best service. It's no bargain to find an inexpensive ISP if you have trouble getting connected to its service because the line is always busy. Want some advice? Find someone who is happy with his service and follow his lead.

It's always a good idea to know what questions to ask before buying anything. Consider the following points when you're shopping for an ISP.

Does the ISP have a local number for your area? You need to call the provider each time you access the Internet. Paying a toll call every time you do so will cost you a ton of money if you use the Internet regularly.

Can the system handle a large number of simultaneous connections? Ask them how many users they can handle at one time and how many subscribers they have. Although they may have a reasonable price and a local number, it doesn't mean much if you can't get on to use it. If after you subscribe you find that you are never able to connect or that the only available access is late at night or early in the morning, then find a new ISP.

Do they offer SLIP/PPP connections? This is the type of connection that you'll need if you want to use a graphical browser like Navigator or Internet Explorer. Some ISP's offer only shell accounts, which require you to type in each command as you would with DOS. It is somewhat like driving a horse and buggy when everyone else has an automobile.

Is monthly subscription fee reasonable? Cheapest is not always best. Added features and staffing support are important points to consider when choosing a service. Some ISP's offer you unlimited monthly connection time at a flat fee, and others offer you a per-hour fee with additional hours costing extra. You will need to estimate your expected usage and purchase accordingly. Ask if there is a fee to upgrade your service if you find that you need more time. If you have a roommate, then consider upgrading the service and splitting the cost. This may actually save you money.

Does your ISP include the Internet browser software in the price? You'll find that not all do. Most ISP's have an agreement with either Netscape or Microsoft to bundle their browser software. The provided software may also be partially configured to work on the ISP's system, so you'll be much farther along by using it and the technicians will be better able to help you with a problem.

Is the ISP a regional or local company? This may not be important to everyone, but some of you may go home during holidays or travel far and wide during vacations, and your destinations may be quite far from campus. If the ISP covers a wide enough area, you can still check your e-mail and cruise the Net when you are away from school.

Do they have a help line in case you need technical assistance to set up your connection? Call the help line before subscribing and make sure to get a real person. Although you may be asked to leave your name and number, you should expect to get a return call within 24 hours. If they don't return your call within this time period, then the service is probably understaffed or poorly managed.

Does the ISP offer both newsgroup and e-mail access in addition to a connection to the Web? This is usually standard, but there are always exceptions. It's better to ask up front.

Does it cost you extra for additional e-mail addresses? If you have a roommate, then you may find that it is more affordable to split the cost of a subscription and pay for an additional e-mail account.

Will your ISP add newsgroups at your request? Most ISP's subscribe to a small fraction of the available news groups, and you may find that they don't include some of the basic, business and economics-oriented groups that your instructors may recommend. It shouldn't cost anything for the ISP to add these groups to their list.

Does the ISP offer you space for your own Web page? Often, one of the features offered in the basic package is the option of constructing and posting your own Web page. The ISP usually sets a memory usage limit that affects the total size of the page and its traffic flow (that is, the number of people viewing the site).

The most important thing to remember when using an ISP is to expect courteous and prompt service. If you don't like what you are paying for, then cancel and go somewhere else. There are plenty of competitors willing to offer you better service.

What sort of ISP should a business consider?

Business users pay significantly more per month because they connect at a higher speed. As prices for Internet connections for businesses are also in free fall, it makes little sense to enter into contracts for longer than one year. Because the price increases with the speed of the connection, it is best to buy less bandwidth initially as long as you can increase speed in the future without significant upgrade penalties. Advice for businesses? Hire a reputable management team to design your network, negotiate with vendors, and see the project through to completion. This way when something goes wrong (and it always does) it is the management team's problem and not yours.

Why are there mistakes in this book?

They changed their Web site, that's why! home pages change. This **will** happen to you somewhere in this book. So, what should you do?

One thing that might help is to remember the path system used in Web page naming. Suppose you visit the site: **www.cc.gatech.edu/gvu/user_surveys**. Recall that the first part (**www.cc.gatech.edu**) identifies the host computer at that site. All pages at the site are contained in folders (subdirectories) of the host computer. For example, suppose the information you need is in the **gvu/user_surveys** folder. Fortunately, you rarely need to know in which subdirectory the information you are searching for is contained. A well-designed site will have a home page on the host computer at the top level (**www.cc.gatech.edu**) with links to all the pages on the site. So if **www.cc.gatech.edu/gvu/user_surveys** is not bringing you the information that you require, then simply back up to **www.cc.gatech.edu** and work your way down by following the links.

Another thing to remember is that there are many sources for some types of information. If something changes, try using search engines to find another source that will answer your questions. This step will really increase your surfing skills.

By the way, being able to change a home page is good. Content providers can continually update their pages and change graphics to make them more useful, without bearing the heavy costs of printed materials. They can experiment with new ideas at low cost and keep things fresh so consumers will be enticed to return.

How do I know that an online source is credible?

You don't. Just because information is on the Internet doesn't mean that it's complete, accurate, or objective. Before you use data from any online source, ask:

What do you know about the source? When in doubt, seek out online sources that have a reputation for reliability. Many Web sites are sponsored by well-known organizations, such as major newspapers, that have earned a reputation for integrity. On the other hand, some Web sites don't even identify their sponsors. So be wary if the source is completely unfamiliar or has a questionable reputation.

Does the source seem biased? Think about whether the source is likely to have a definite point of view on certain issues. For example, when you browse the Web site of the American Association of Retired Persons, bear in mind that the information is likely to reflect that group's role as an advocate for people over 50 years old. Knowing the organization's purpose and viewpoint can help you interpret any information you use from that source.

What is the original source of the information? In many cases, Web sites and databases draw their information from other sources, such as government studies. If the original source is noted, take time to evaluate its reputation and potential for bias before you use the data. If no original source is indicated, approach the data with caution.

Can you verify the source's information? Before you use information from an online source, try to find another source to verify the data. You can use a search tool such as Infoseek or Metacrawler to scan the Internet for the same kind of data provided by at least one other reliable source. The ability to confirm information serves as a valuable check on the data's accuracy—and the accuracy of its source.

Does the source's information seem reasonable to you? As a final check on any online source, use your judgment to evaluate the data and the conclusions. Given the other facts you have uncovered on the subject, does this source's information seem unreasonable or out of line? If so, it's time to find a better source.

How does plagiarism apply to information from online sources?

Online research is so convenient that you may be tempted simply to copy material from an Internet source and paste it intact within your document. However, unless your sources are properly documented, you will be plagiarizing. Whether you're working on a term paper or researching a business report, you should cite your source when you (1) quote word-for-word, (2) closely paraphrase, or (3) repeat a series of phrases from documents posted on the Internet. This includes news articles, books or excerpts, surveys, speeches, transcripts of online discussions, manuals, and any material on Web pages sponsored by individuals, corporations, schools, nonprofit groups, or government agencies. When in doubt, you can avoid even the hint of plagiarism by fully documenting your sources. Internet sources for information on how to handle Internet references is provided in Chapter 5.

So where do I go for more information?

If you'd like to know more about the workings and history of the Internet – it's a fascinating story of trial and error, discovery, and flashes of true genius – we recommend the following books and Web sites:

Books

Internet in a Nutshell: A Desktop Quick Reference by Valerie Quercia
O'Reilly & Associates Inc.

The Whole Internet for Windows 95 : User's Guide & Catalog by Paula Ferguson, Ed. Krol
O'Reilly & Associates

A Student's Guide to the Internet by Carol Lea Clark
Prentice Hall

Where Wizards Stay up Late: The Origins of the Internet by Katie Hafner and Matthew Lyon
Simon and Schuster

World Wide Web Sites

World Wide Web Consortium
This is a group at MIT that is the focal point for changes, additions, and new uses for the World Wide Web. The Web is not "owned" by anyone, but this organization provides continuity and consistency by overseeing changes. From here you can go to any of several Web-related sites.

http://www.w3.org/pub/WWW/

Home Page for Tim Berners-Lee, the Developer of the Web
This is a biography of the man who started it all from the Particle Physics Laboratory (CERN) in Switzerland.

http://www.w3.org/pub/WWW/People/Berners-Lee-Bio.html/

Netscape's and Microsoft's Home Pages
The Netscape and Microsoft Web sites are excellent sources for information about the Web and for software to get the most from the Web. You can use the following Internet addresses to research the right browser for you. You can also download the latest version of Netscape Navigator or Internet Explorer (the two most popular Web browsers) from these sites free of charge.

http://home.netscape.com/
http://www.microsoft.com/

Information on Internet Service Providers

With your computer, modem, and browser, you're now only one step away from the Web. Earlier we pointed out that both Netscape and Yahoo! provide lists of ISPs. However a simple list does not provide you with the information you need to choose among the various options. Use the following Internet addresses to research the right ISP for you. You might want to consider the questions outlined earlier.

Choosing An Internet Provider
http://tcp.ca/Dec95/Commtalk_ToC.html

Internet Access Provider Guide
http://www.liii.com/~dhjordan/students/docs/welcome.htm

Choosing the Internet Service Provider - Netscape
http://home.netscape.com/assist/isp_select/index.html

Computer Magazines

It is always nice to have an independent opinion. Read what the critics have to say. Stop by the following Internet addresses, and visit the largest publishers of computer-related magazines. Altogether, these companies print nearly 50 different popular periodicals about computers and the Internet. Search their databases for articles that will help you make the most of your Internet experience. You can read the articles online.

CMP Media Inc.'s (Publisher of *Windows Magazine* and others)
http://www.techweb.com/info/publications/publications.html

Ziff Davis (Publisher of *PC Magazine*, *MacUser*, and others)
http://www5.zdnet.com/findit/search.html

Chapter 2
Up and Running: The Search is On

Let's look now at how to use the browser for navigating the Internet. First we discuss basic navigation techniques. Then we show you how to conduct searches on the Internet.

Cruising the Net

Although the Internet may seem large and disorganized, finding your way around can be easier than finding your way to a friend's house. Information on the Internet has an address just as your friend does. Most browsers allow you to type in an address and access information from, or "go to", a particular document.

Let's take a look at how to enter an address using each of the most popular Web browsers, Netscape Navigator and Microsoft Internet Explorer, shown in Figure 2.1. Start by finding the text entry box, to the right of the words *Go to* or *Address*. (Sometimes the words *Location* or *Netsite* appear instead.) In either browser you may type in the address and press the return button on your keyboard. Be sure to type in the address accurately. Even one mistake will prevent you from making the connection you want. Alternatively you can press the *Ctrl* and *"O"* keys and an *Open Page* box will appear. Type in the address.

Now take a look at the row of icons directly above the text box. This is known as the *Navigation Tool Bar*. Clicking on an individual icon causes the computer to execute the command noted below the icon.

How do each of these commands help you to navigate the Internet? In Figure 2.1, find the button labeled *Back*–it's at the far left. By clicking on this button you can return to the Web page you just visited. If you have gone to many Web pages, you can use the Back button repeatedly to return to your starting point.

Now find the *Home* button. By selecting this button, you will immediately return to the home page configured for your browser. When you first begin using your browser, it will be set to a page determined by the company that created it. At some point you may want to change your home page or even create your own. But for now, remember that you can always go home.

Two other buttons common to most browsers are *Stop* and *Reload* (or *Refresh*). The *Stop* button stops your computer from linking to the address that you have just asked for. *Reload* needs just a bit more explanation. As you explore more of the Internet, you'll realize that complete pages don't show up in your browser window instantly. Instead, different types of elements (pictures, icons, text, animations, and so on) appear over time as they are moved from the server to your browser. Occasionally, you'll notice that a page loads without some of these elements. This is often caused by an error in the transmission. Use the *Reload* button to request a new copy of the page. Additionally, browsers keep a copy of the images and text from sites you have visited in a file known as the cache. Often a browser will load the file from the cache rather than from the source. If the source has been recently changed you will likely not get the most recent version. Pressing the *Reload* or *Refresh* button will force the browser to go to the source and get the new information.

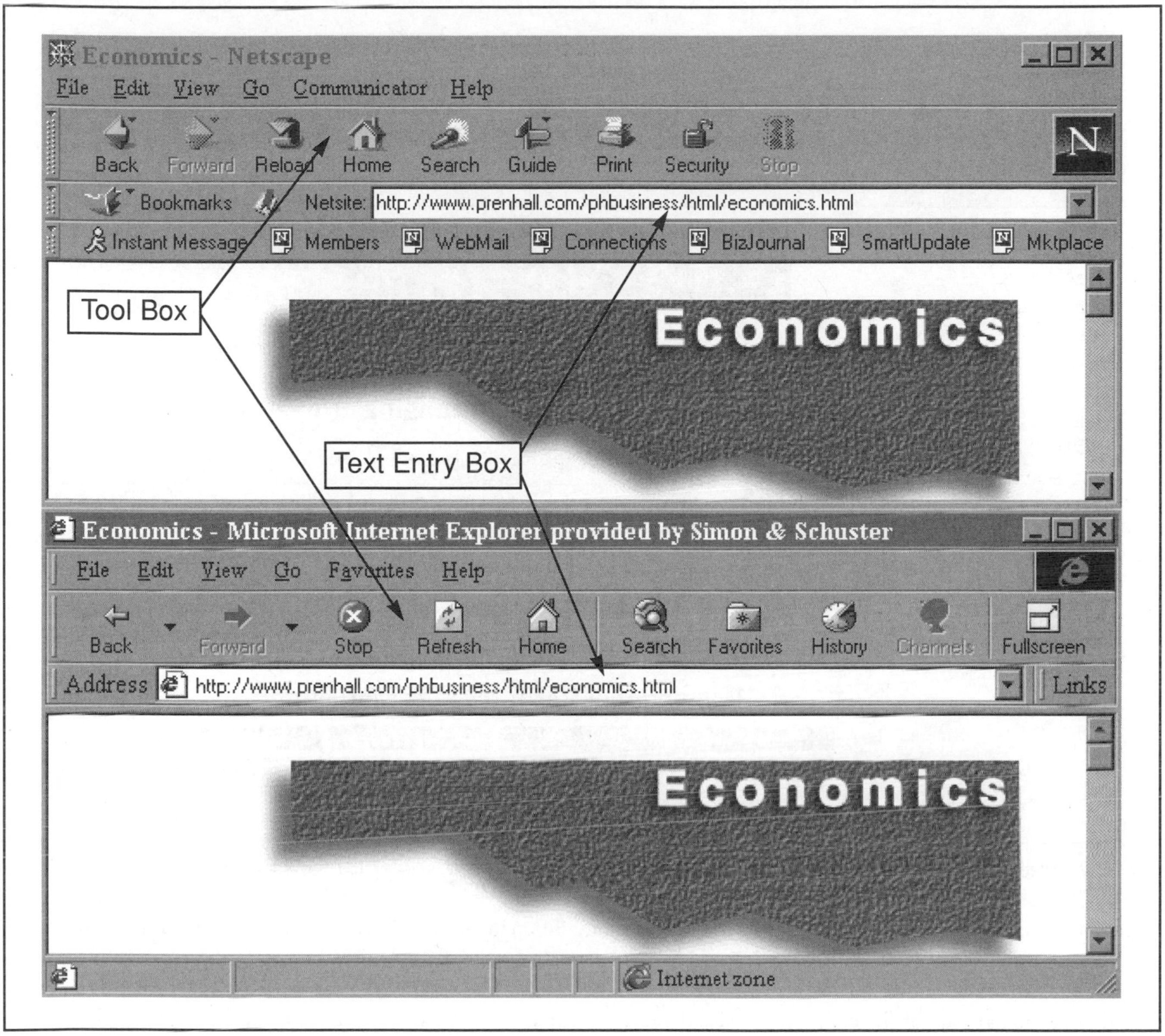

Figure 2.1. The tool bar for both Netscape Navigator and Microsoft Internet Explorer offer basic navigation features such as **Back**, **Forward**, and **Home**. You will find everything you'll need to perform simple navigation around the Internet.

To make life a bit easier, we will use Netscape Navigator as the browser in illustrations from this point on. If you are using Internet Explorer, you should find the instructions easy to translate. After all, the basic functions of a browser are much the same from one to another. For those interested in the specifics, we are using Netscape Communicator 4.04, a package of programs including the latest version of Netscape Navigator.

You don't always have to know the address of a page to view that page. The wonderful thing about the Web is that you can access (navigate) pages through the use of hyperlinks. You will notice that hyperlinks are often colored words (typically blue) on a Web page. Images may also be hyperlinks. Click your mouse on the desired hyperlink, and you will travel to a new Web page, just as you would if you typed in an address (see Figure 2.2).

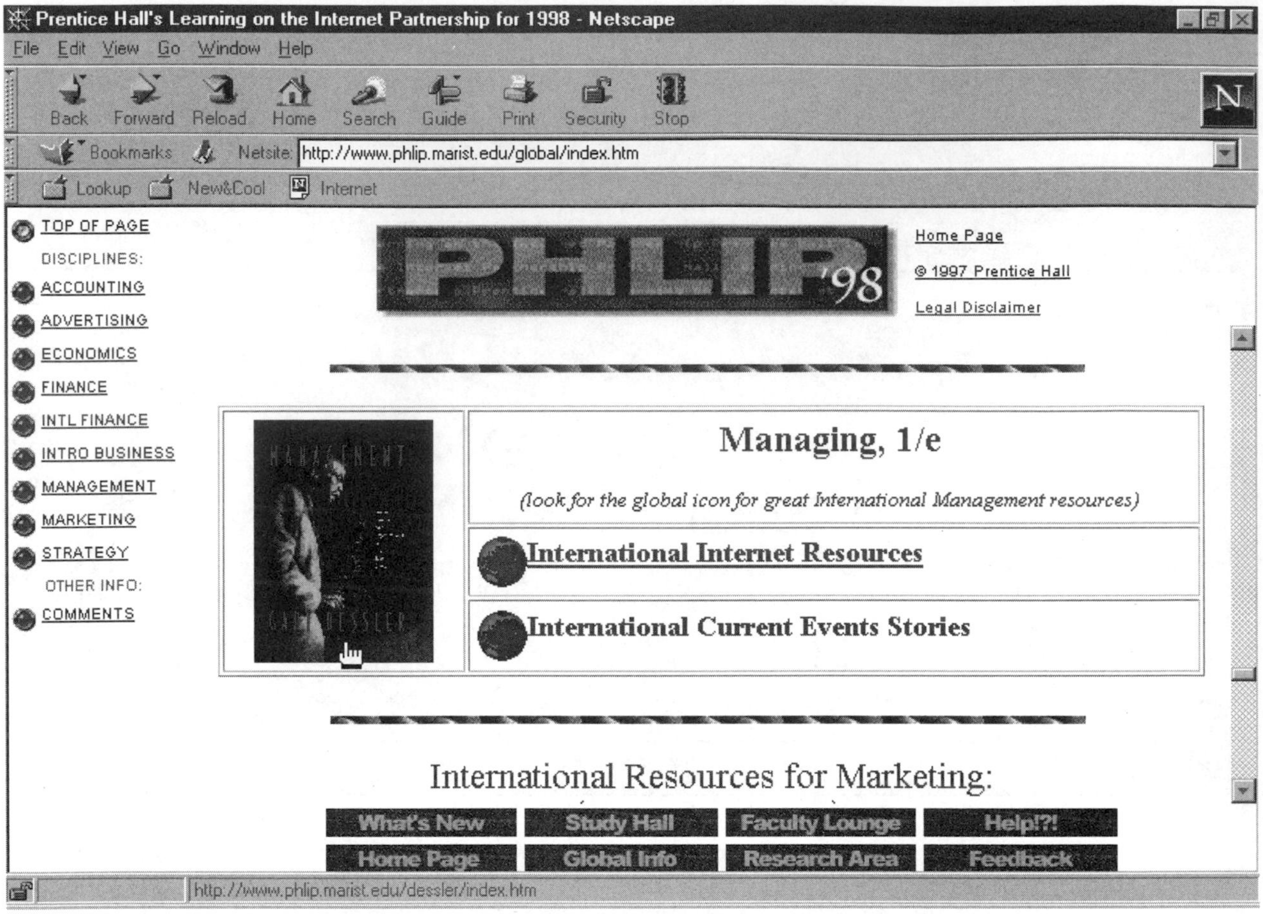

Figure 2.2 Hyperlinks can be words or images. Note that the cursor, on the image, is now a hand, indicating that it is a hyperlink.

The author of a Web page can connect one image to many different places. This type of hyperlink is sometimes called a clickable map. For example, think of a Web page with a map of the United States. For any place you might want more information on, just point your mouse to it and click! You are linked to another location with more details on that particular part of the country. Go ahead and try it for yourself by visiting the sites in the following box.

Here are two addresses that use clickable maps. Both of these use an actual map for the clickable map.

City.Net Travel
    http://city.net/countries/united_states/
U.S. Census Bureau
    http://www.census.gov/datamap/www/

Note that clickable maps do not necessarily need to be in a format of a traditional "map." Here is a site that uses an image map that is not a map proper.

> Xmorphia
> http://www.ccsf.caltech.edu/ismap/image.html

The Xmorphia site is a good example of an image map that serves a very specialized purpose. For the more mathematically inclined, it is a fascinating application. For other people, it's an interesting image. Also note that not all browsers support clickable maps. However, most good Web authors will provide conventional hyperlinks to related sites in addition to the clickable map.

Some Web pages contain forms. A form is generally a request for information, which you may respond to by clicking with your mouse or typing an answer. Forms can be used to survey users, answer questions, or make requests. If you'd like to see a Web page that uses forms, you might want to visit a college or university admissions office site. Those sites often use forms to develop contacts with prospective students. Another site of particular interest to economics students is maintained by *The Economist* magazine. If you wish to make use of *The Economist* (and it is an excellent source for a wide variety of information), you need to register, and registration is free. If you direct your browser to *The Economist* located at http://www.economist.com/, and then click on the *Register* link (in the left bar), you will have an opportunity to register and use *The Economist.*

Bookmarks

Now that you've found some really interesting pages, how do you find them again a day or a week later without going through the same hassle? Your browser provides a way to mark a site so you can quickly return to it. Netscape calls this feature Bookmarks (see Figure 2.3). With this feature you can compile a list of pages you frequently visit. When you wish to return to one of these pages, you simply select it from the list by clicking on it with your mouse. You will jump directly to the site.

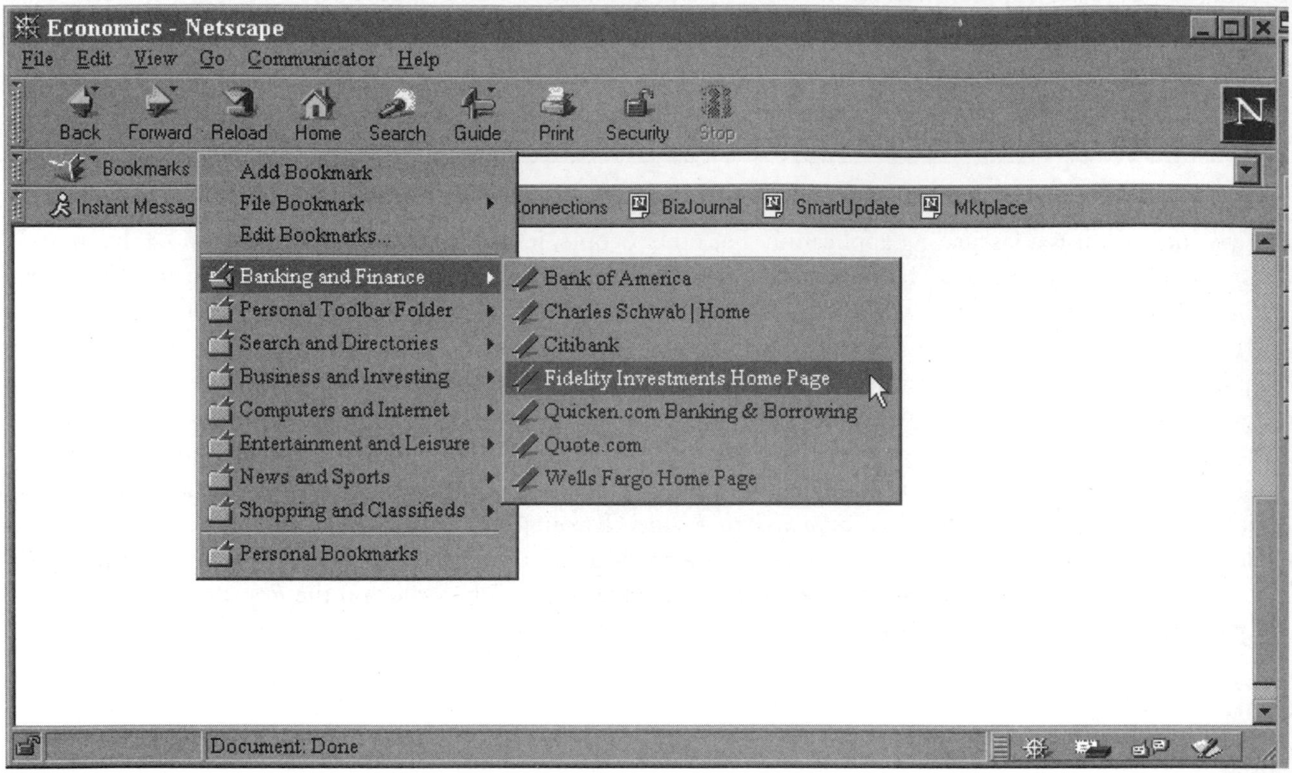

Figure 2.3. As pages are added to this list they will appear at the bottom of this same pull-down menu. In this case the browser is about to go to Fidelity Investments' site.

Here are some addresses to get your bookmark collection started. Go back to The Economist site and add it to your bookmarks. To save this site, select Add Bookmark from the Bookmarks menu (see Figure 2.3). Then go to Resources for Economists, an excellent site for anyone interested in economics. The addresses for these sites are:

> *The Economist*
> http://www.economist.com/
>
> Resources for Economists on the Internet
> http://econwpa.wustl.edu/EconFAQ/EconFAQ.html

Later on, if you use your mouse to select the *Bookmarks* menu, you'll see that both *The Economist* and Resources for Economists on the Internet are just a jump away. You don't have to memorize the addresses or haphazardly jump around until you find them again.

Most of you will be working from a computer lab as well as from your own computer. You can save your bookmarks file to a disk and carry it around with you. To do this, follow the *Edit Bookmarks* link in the Bookmarks menu and select *Save As* under the *File* menu. Then enter the drive and filename where you wish them saved. (As a matter of fact, it is not a bad idea to create a small Web page on a disk and keep it with you so that from any computer you can load your "traveling home page" and have your links handy. More on how to do this at the end of Chapter 3 in the section on creating Web pages.)

As you begin to accumulate more sites, you'll notice how cluttered and disorganized your list can become. Most browsers allow you to organize bookmarks as you desire. Let's assume you have a rich list of business-related bookmarks, and you want to put them in order. From the *Bookmarks* menu, select *Edit Bookmarks* and then select *File*. From this menu, select *New Folder*. You will then be prompted to type in a name and description(optional) for your new folder. Perhaps you want to add a folder for microeconomics. Type MicroEcon, then click *OK*. You then just click on whatever addresses you want to add in this folder and drag them to that folder name.

To view what is in a particular folder, just click on *Bookmarks* and place the cursor on the folder name. A menu will pop up with a list of the bookmarks you've stored there.

For Web sites that you access on a regular basis, you can create a button (hyperlink) on the *Personal Toolbar* by just clicking on the icon to the right of *Bookmarks* and dragging it to the *Personal Toolbar*. You have to be visiting the Web site at the time to create this link.

Go and History

If you've been working along with this guide and your browser at the same time, you've probably been to many places on the Web. If you are moving back and forth between your selections, you are probably using the Forward and Back buttons on the browser toolbar. But what if you want to go back fifteen jumps? Do you press the Back button fifteen times? Well, that works, but it is a little slow. You might want to try a different approach, which allows you to jump rapidly to any of the places you've visited along your path of travel. In Navigator, select the *Go* menu. You'll see a list of all of the places you've visited on your journey. Select the appropriate site, and away you go. You might also use *History*, which appears under the *Communicator* (or *Window* on older versions) menu. You'll open a new window listing the names and the addresses for all of the places you've been to recently. Other browsers have similar features.

Because the list compiled under *Go* begins anew each time you start your browser and the *History* file is kept for only a few days (nine is the default), you should still use *Bookmarks* when you find something interesting. Another way of going back to somewhere you've been is to select the "down triangle" button to the right of the *Text Entry Box* (it is just below the Netscape "N" in Figure 2.3). You will see all the sites you have typed directly in the Text Entry Box.

Asking for Directions

The Internet is truly vast. It contains plenty of valuable information, but it's not always easy to find what you need. To help you find your way, however, a number of easy-to-use tools are available for free. With practice, these tools will help you develop better information-finding skills. Our next section offers a look at how to streamline your journeys through the Net.

Search Strategies

Let's focus now on search techniques that will help you find the information you need on the Web. Some of the search techniques are very basic. Others take some time to master. It is worth learning all these search techniques because they will increase your Net research efficiency and effectiveness.

We turn to Open Text and Subject Tree searches. Open text searches scan the Web looking for a word or group of words you have entered as your search string. The search engine then lists links to pages on the Web that it determines are most relevant to your search string. A page with more matches is considered more likely to be relevant.

A subject tree search takes a different approach. A subject tree is a catalog of a great number of pages on the Web, neatly organized by category, sub-category, sub-sub-category, and so on. For example, suppose you wanted to look into the economics of selling athletic wear. You could follow any number of paths, and we'll give you one example here that you could find with Yahoo!, which we'll explain soon:

Business ➪ Companies ➪ Apparel ➪ Athletic Wear ➪ Footwear ➪ Brand Names ➪ Nike

There you are. Along the way, as you read through the various sub-categories, you may develop new ideas for what information you want to find and how you'll get to it. Users navigate down through the subject tree until they reach a link pointing to a page that looks relevant. There is more work involved in a subject tree search than in an open text search, but the results are often worth the effort. We generally recommend beginning with a subject tree search for three reasons. First, people – not robot programs -- compile subject trees, and these people cut out links that are useless. Second, subject trees help orient your search by showing you which sites fall into the same category. This grouping may lead you to discover sources of information that you had not considered. Third, the premier subject tree index, Yahoo!, is very good.

Indeed Yahoo! is actually a bit of a hybrid between subject tree and open text searches. In addition to offering the ability to drill down manually, there is also a search feature on Yahoo! that shows you all categories matching your search term. Furthermore, after showing you its own matches, Yahoo! also offers you the option of transferring your search to AltaVista (another, more detailed search engine) for even more matches.

Why so many search engines?

Let's consider Yahoo! (a subject tree) and AltaVista (open text search). A couple of graduate school dropouts from Stanford created Yahoo!. AltaVista has corporate roots: Digital Equipment started it. The two engines have a unique relationship since Yahoo! will pass along an open text search to AltaVista for processing. So why use anything else? Well, like all products in the service sector, each search engine has unique features. Some catalog a greater percentage of the Web, some are faster, some have more advanced search features, some are geared toward a specialized area of information, and some will translate your words into a concept and then search for the concept. There are even meta search engines that simultaneously feed your query to multiple search engines for processing. The latest approach to search engines is provided by Alexa, at **www.alexa.com**. This is not a search engine proper but a program that runs with your browser and provides you with constant updates on where you are, tells you how the site you are currently visiting is rated, and suggests where to go next by giving you a set of links related to the one you are currently visiting. In addition to the running information, Alexa is linked to an archive of the Web so that you can visit sites that are no longer available. The best approach is to learn how to use one or two search engines well and then generalize your knowledge to other search engines as needed. If you have a burning desire to learn more about search engines, visit this site, which is devoted to keeping up with search engines: The Search Engine Watch at http://searchenginewatch.com/.

Subject Tree Index

A subject tree, as we have pointed out, is an index to the World Wide Web organized by categories and sub-categories. The most comprehensive subject tree index on the Web is Yahoo!. Try it out! You can reach Yahoo! in three different ways:

- Type in the address in the *Text Entry Box*
- Press *Ctrl-O* and enter the address in the *Open Page* box (see figure 2.4)
- Click on the *Search* button located on the Navigation Toolbar. One of the choices is Yahoo!

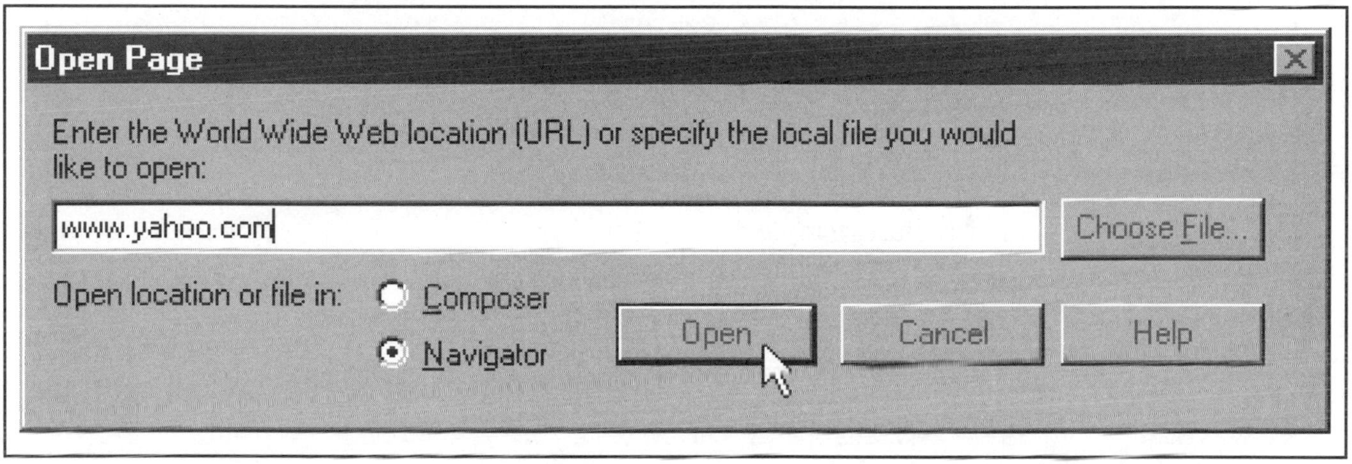

Figure 2.4 Typing an Internet address in the Open Page box is just one of three ways Netscape provides for you to access a site on the Web.

To start Yahoo! you need first to launch your Web browser. To get to Yahoo!'s site you type: http://www.yahoo.com/ in the *Address* or *Location* line of your browser and then press the return key. Some of the top level Yahoo! categories appear in Figure 2.5:

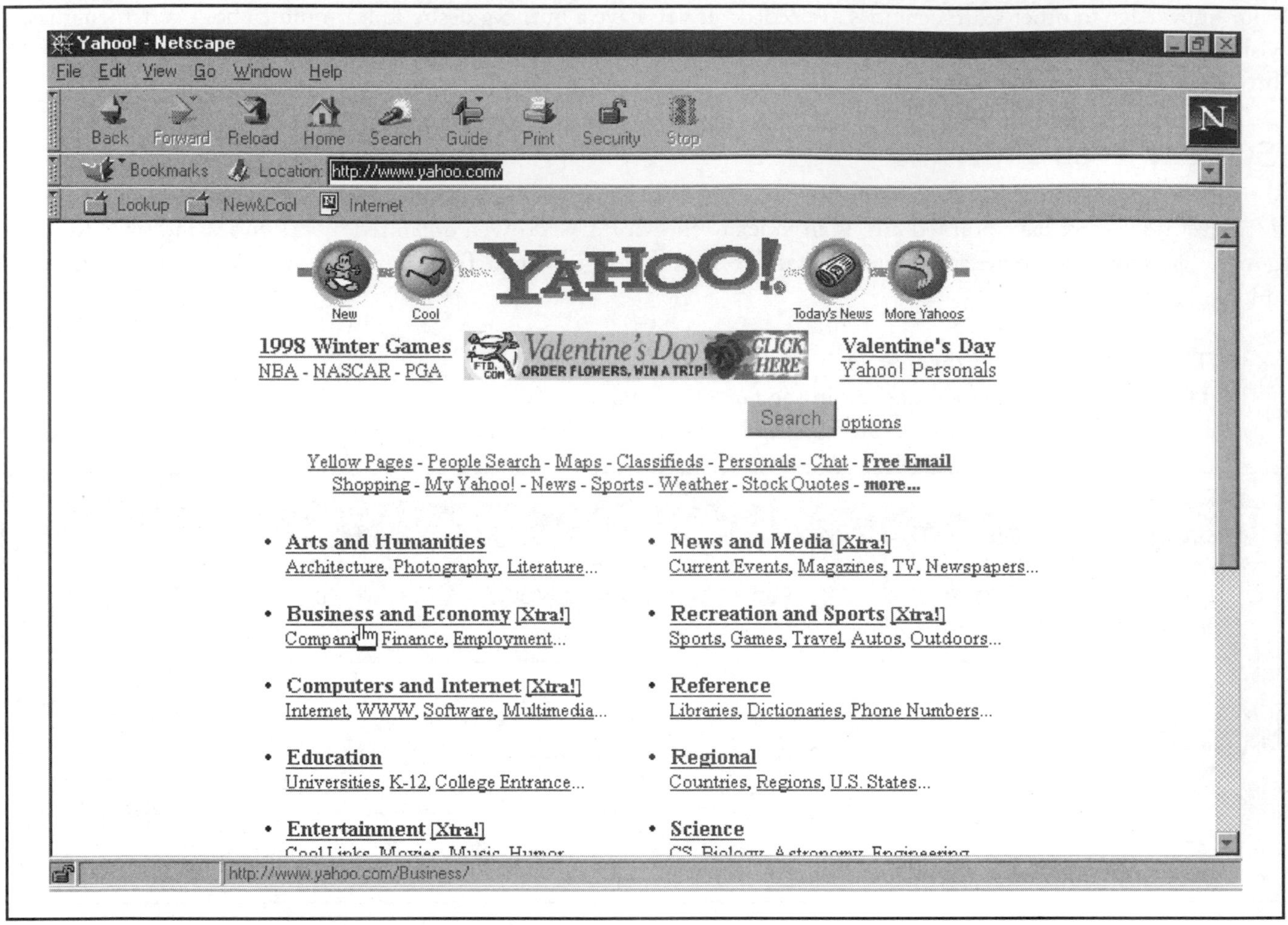

Figure 2.5 Yahoo! is the most comprehensive subject tree index on the Web.

To explore the business category more in depth click on *Business and Economy*. This brings up a list of all of the business and economics sub-categories, which looks like this:

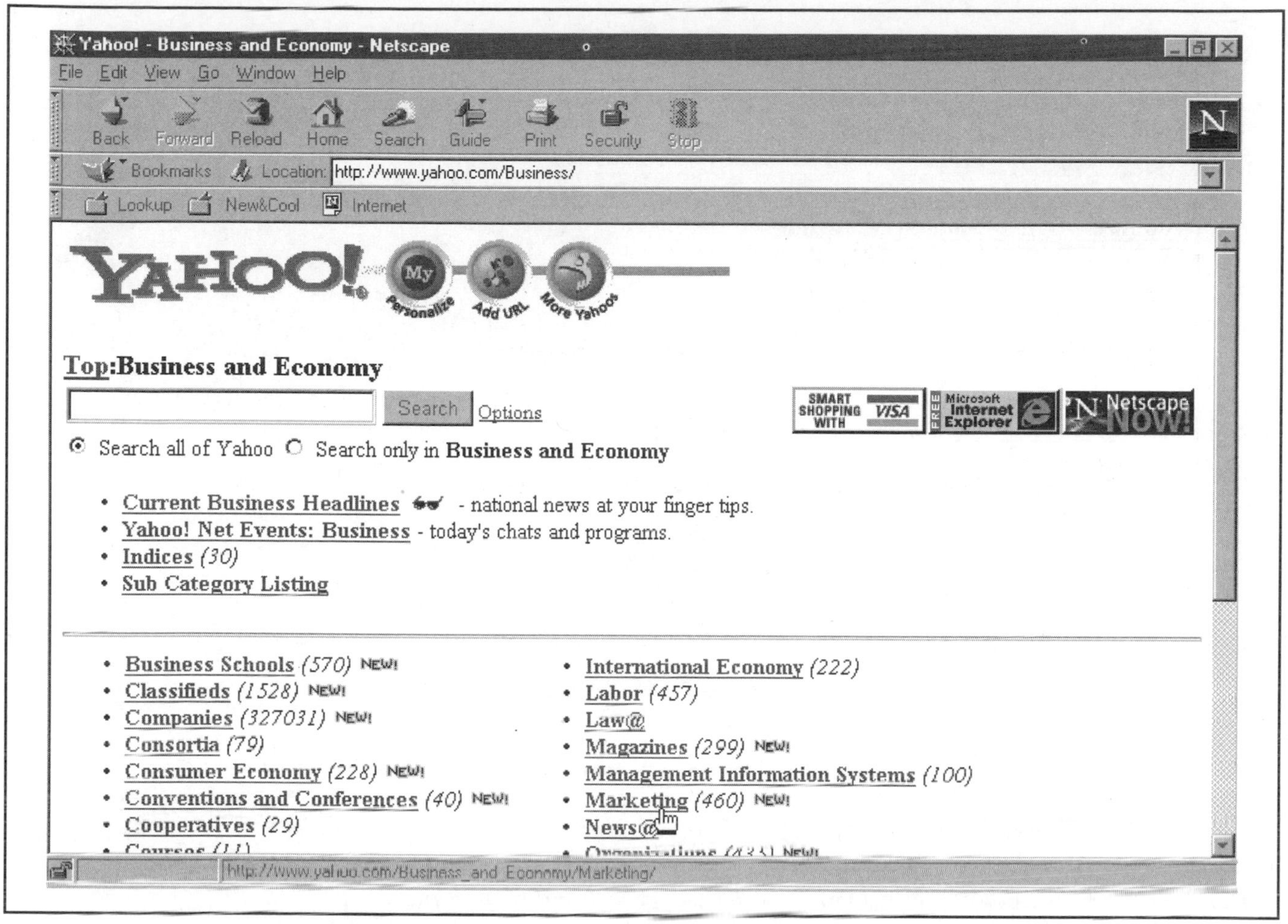

Figure 2.6 By digging down through sub-categories, a subject tree search allows you to search for specific information on any given topic.

Yahoo! boldfaces sub-categories as well as indicates the number of entries in parentheses. For example we know that the Marketing sub-category contains 460 entries, some of which are relatively new. To explore the Marketing category more in depth click on *Marketing* and you will see:

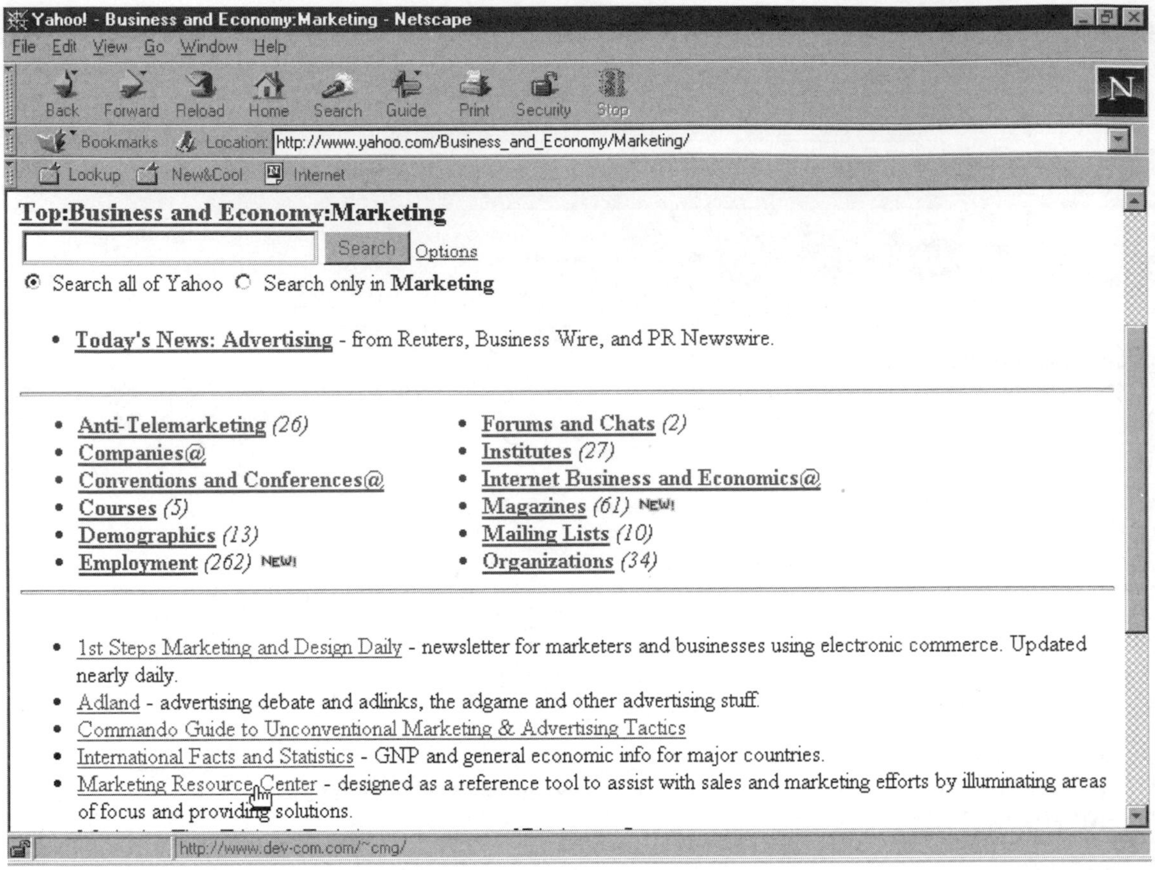

Figure 2.7 Below the sub-categories, Yahoo! lists direct links to other Web sites that might be of interest to you.

At this level we see that there are further sub-categories such as Demographics, Employment, and Organizations. Below these sub-categories we also see entries that are direct links to marketing-related sites on the Internet. For example, by clicking on *Marketing Resource Center* we are lead directly to a wealth of information along with hyperlinks to other marketing related sites (see Figure 2.8).

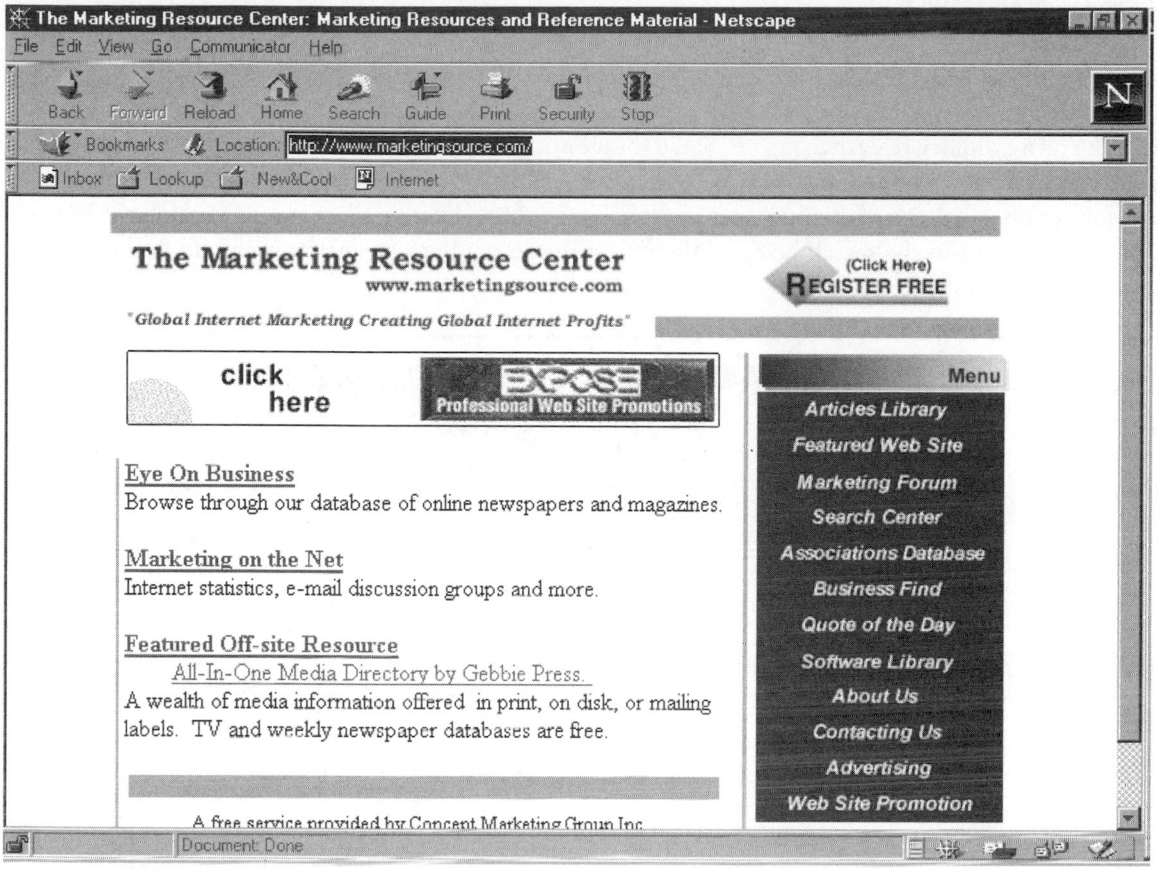

Figure 2.8 The Marketing Resource Center page is one step on an infinite path of hyperlink connections.

Note how for the first time the address has changed so that we are no longer on Yahoo!'s site. We have followed a link off of Yahoo!'s index to another site somewhere else in the world.

Your Turn

Using the Yahoo! subject tree index, locate the site that contains the entire text of Adam Smith's *An Inquiry into the Nature and Causes of the Wealth of Nations* (or just *The Wealth of Nations* for short). Begin at the top level and scroll down until you find a direct link. Because economics is a social science and is the parent of the academic study of business, you can begin at either of these top-levels.

How many levels did you have to drill down to reach the site?
What other links along the way look like they might be worth exploring?

Open Text Search

An open text search is a keyword search through the entire Web. All pages matching the keywords are returned by the search engine and then ranked in order of relevance. Generally, pages containing the keywords the greatest number of times are given a higher relevance rating. Since thousands of documents can contain the same keywords it is important for you to be as specific as possible in your search.
Yahoo! incorporates open text searching in two ways (see Figure 2.9). First, it allows you to search the entire Yahoo! site when you enter a term in the search box and then press the search button. For example, if we enter Nike in the search box, we get the following results:

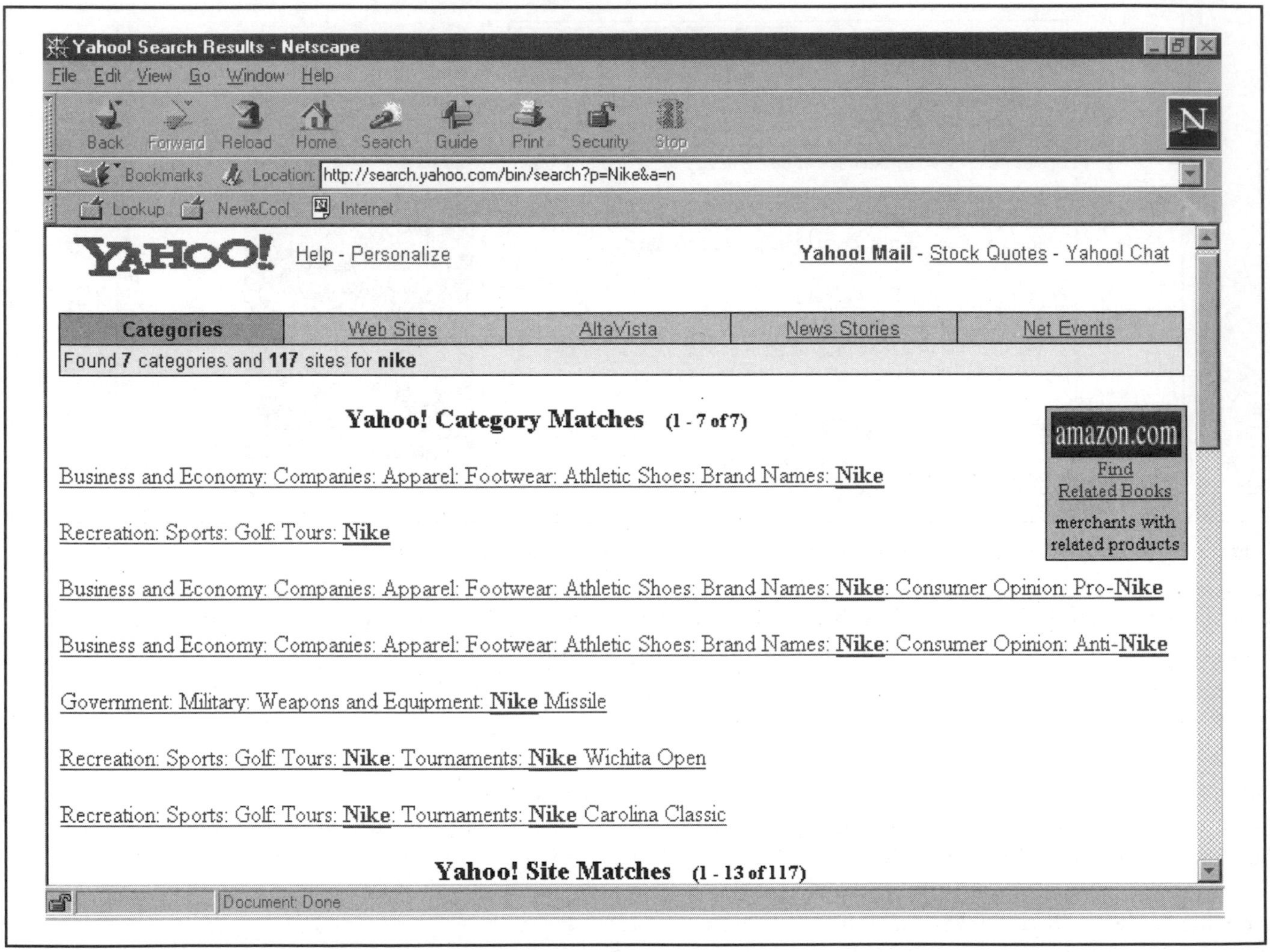

Figure 2.9 Yahoo! also allows you to do an open text search.

This tells us that Yahoo! has seven categories under which Nike is listed. Additionally, it has categorized links to 117 different sites that contain information about the company.

Second, Yahoo! allows us to transfer our search to AltaVista if none of the links are useful (see Figure 2.10).

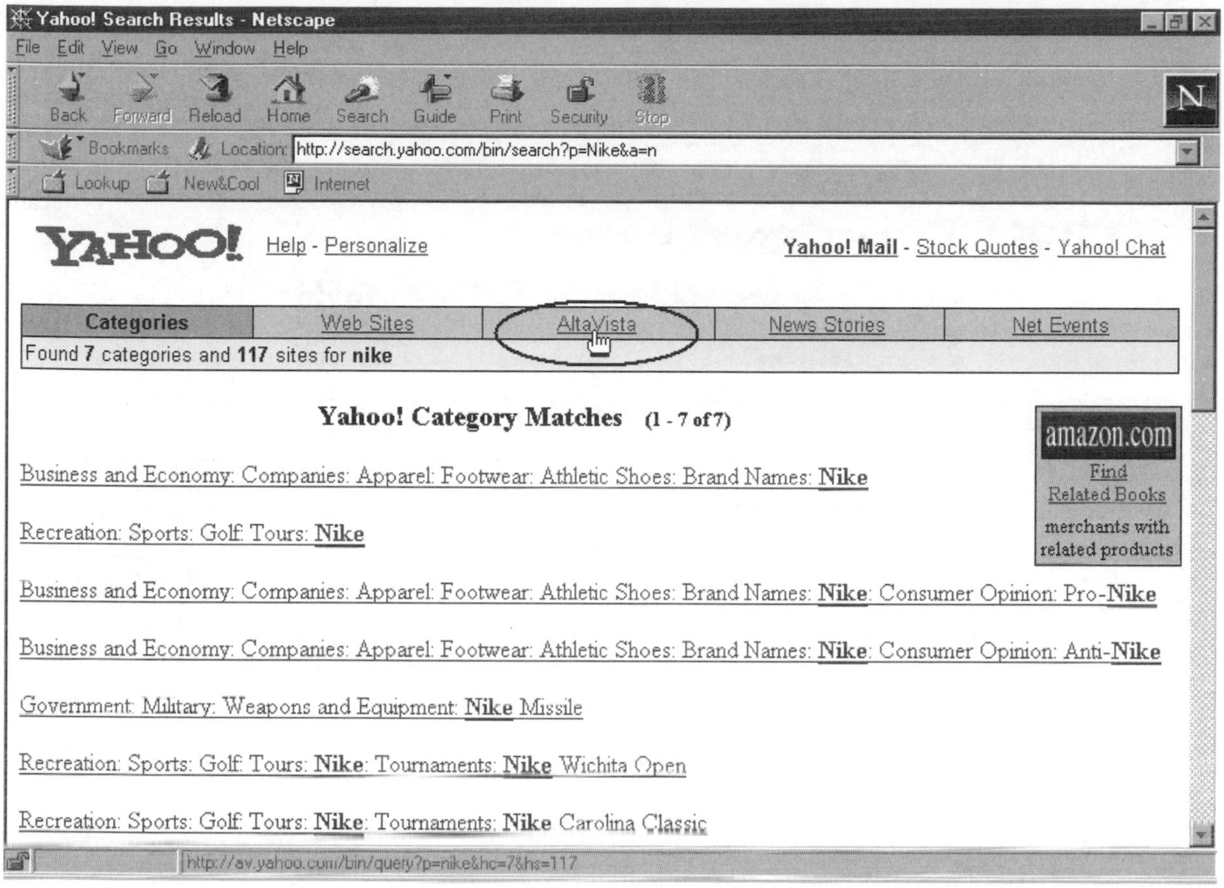

Figure 2.10 If the result of your Yahoo! search is insufficient, additional search results are just a click away with Yahoo's! direct link to AltaVista.

By clicking on the AltaVista item our search is transferred to AltaVista and the results look like this:

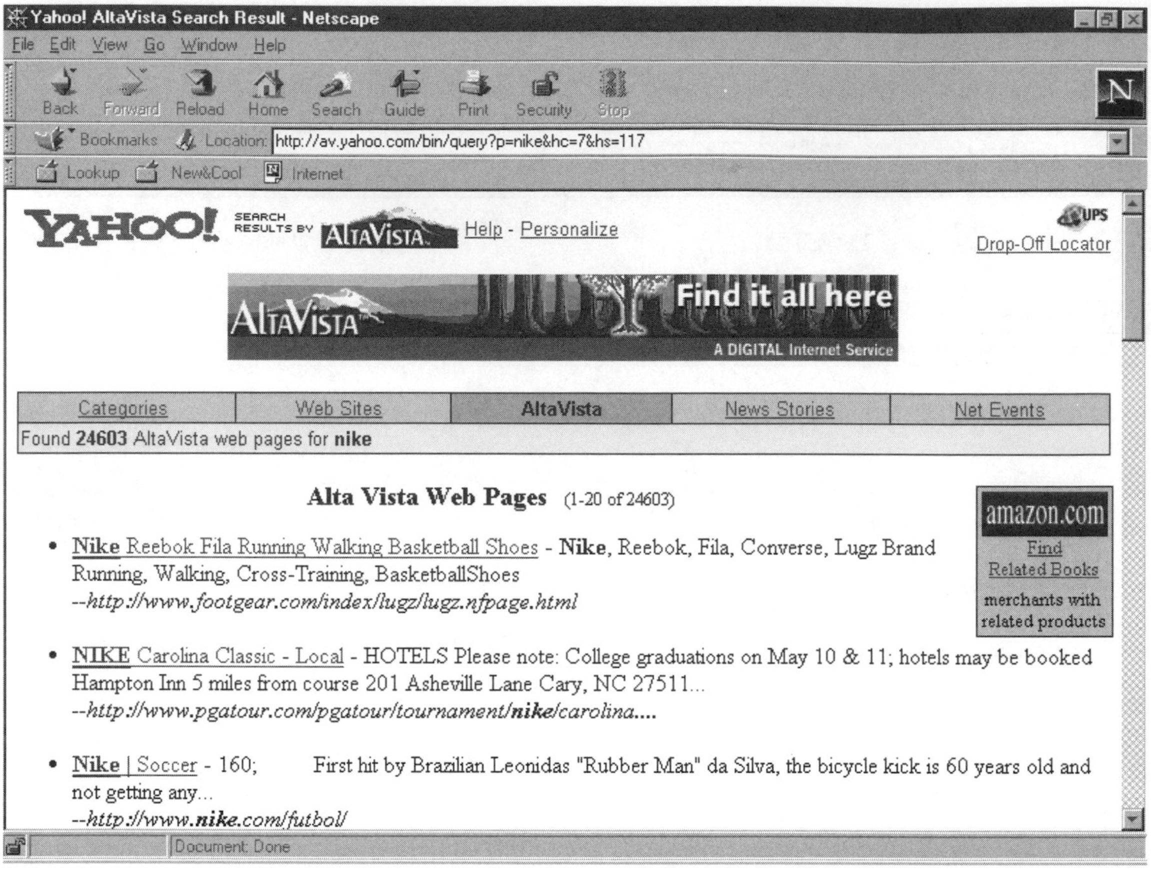

Figure 2.11 AltaVista has come up with a much greater number of related Web sites (24,603 vs. 117) with an open text search, but more is not always better. If you know what you are looking for, it would be more productive to fine tune your results through a category search. (DIGITAL, AltaVista, and the AltaVista logo are trademarks or service marks of Digital Equipment Corporation. Used in permission.)

Note that AltaVista has found 24,603 Web pages that mention Nike. The first 20 matches are displayed on the page. The first one shown is supposed to be the most relevant. But is it? Can you begin to see why we like you to start with Yahoo!?

Your Turn

Using the Yahoo! open text search feature, conduct the three searches in the following table, which progressively narrow down a subject. Record the number of matches given with each search string.

Keywords Searched for	Number of Yahoo! category matches	Number of Yahoo! site matches	Number of AltaVista pages
interest			
interest rate			
interest rate offered			

What conclusions can you draw from this experiment?

Sometimes the keywords appear on the same page but with hundreds of words separating them. This results in a list of irrelevant sites. Open text searches also incorporate ways to demand that the words not only have to appear on the same page but also must be right next to one another. The easiest way to accomplish this is to put the words that must appear together in quotes. The best way to understand this point is to try it out.

Try an open text search for midwest economic forecast.

How relevant are your search results?
Now try an open text search for midwest "economic forecast."
How relevant is the information returned? Propose an explanation for the difference in results.

Knowing which words to put in quotes is not always obvious since there are times when the keywords never appear next to each other. Try an open text search for "midwest economic forecast."

Did you get any results?

We hope you're starting to feel comfortable traveling the Net. We're going to move now to advanced search techniques.

Advanced Search

Sometimes a simple search turns up rather strange results. In the basic search exercise we saw how quotes could be helpful in limiting the results to useful information. We now introduce some powerful operators that will help you save tremendous amounts of time when searching the Web.

The basic search exercise introduced the Yahoo! search engine. When you performed an open text search in that exercise, the engine first searched the Yahoo! subject tree, showed you Yahoo!'s results, and then passed along the search to AltaVista and showed you AltaVista's results. The Yahoo! subject tree contains all of the pages that the Yahoo! editors have had time to categorize. And while they have categorized a lot, the Yahoo! subject tree is far from complete. By contrast, AltaVista uses a robot program to search the Web and index documents by keywords. AltaVista's robots work tirelessly day and night, and so they are able to visit millions of pages on the Web and index all the keywords that they find. We present AltaVista in this exercise because it complements Yahoo! and because it is quite fast.

Pluses and Minuses

To search the Web most effectively means being able to specify what you want and what you don't want. In AltaVista a plus means that you want the word to appear on a Web page, and a minus means that you don't. So +inflation -currency gives you all sites that have inflation but no currency. Conversely, -inflation +currency gives you all sites that have no inflation but lots on currency. Ready? Start up AltaVista by entering its address in your Web browser – **www.altavista.digital.com**. You should see a welcome page similar to this:

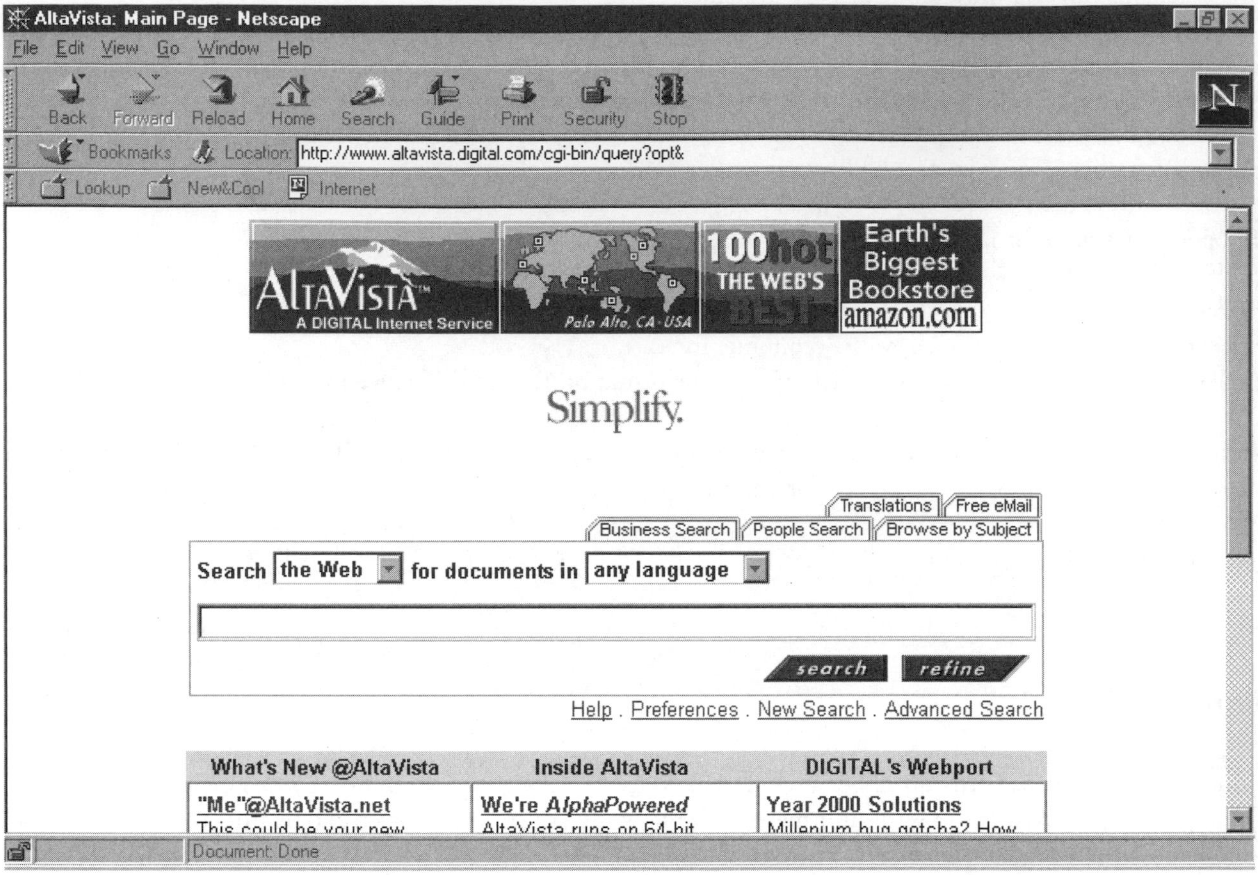

Figure 2.12 AltaVista's home page allows you to refine your open text search on the Web. (DIGITAL, AltaVista, and the AltaVista logo are trademarks or service marks of Digital Equipment Corporation. Used in permission.)

Your Turn

You now enter a search string in the box and then click the button. Let's try our inflation and currency example. Be sure to include a space between the words, or AltaVista will think you are searching for one long word.

You Type	It Means
+inflation -currency	Find all pages that have information on inflation but not currency

About how many documents were returned by the query?
Are you going to read them all? We didn't think so. Now try the second example.

You Type	It Means
-inflation +currency	Find all pages that do not cover inflation but have information on currency

About how many documents were returned by the query?

As you can see, with tens of millions of Web sites covered, AltaVista is going to find a lot of references. Some will be right on target, but most won't be useful to you. AltaVista tries to position the most relevant documents at the top of the list. So how does it determine what's relevant? Generally, AltaVista uses the following criteria to rank a document's relevance:

- the query words or phrases are found in the first few words of the document
- the query words or phrases are found close to one another in the document
- the document contains more than one instance of the query word or phrase

Unfortunately, unscrupulous Web site designers have caught on to these conventions, and some sites overpopulate their sites with keywords so that they appear first in the listings. For example, we once came across a car dealer that repeated Toyota Toyota Toyota... in order to earn a higher relevance rating and thus attract surfers looking for a Toyota site. To filter out these false relevant ratings the better search engines might require, for example, that duplicate instances of keywords be separated by at least seven words.

Keep it Together; Keep it in Quotes

As we said, AltaVista places pages higher on its search results list when the search words appear close together on the Web page. Sometimes you want the search words right next to each other with no words in between. To accomplish this we put the words in quotes.

Your Turn

Let's say we are interested in pages on Web marketing. We'll try typing the words with and without quotes.

You Type	It Means
web marketing	Find all pages that have the words web and marketing

About how many documents did the query find?

Now let's try it with the quotes to force the words to appear right next to each other.

You Type	It Means
"web marketing"	Find all pages that have the words "web" and "marketing" where those words appear right next to each other.

About how many documents did the query find?

Finally, we'll limit your search to just those sites that mention the Nielsen Survey.

You Type	It Means
+"web marketing" +"nielsen survey"	Find all pages that have the words web and marketing where those words appear right next to each other. Those same sites must also have the words "nielsen" and "survey" right next to each other.

About how many documents did the query find?

You can get very specific!

WHEN IN DOUBT, lowercase

You may have noticed that in all of the examples above, we typed the search strings in lowercase letters, even when searching for a proper name such as Nielsen. The reason for this is that lowercase search strings match both lower and uppercase, but uppercase matches uppercase only. So, if some Webmaster forgets to capitalize Nielsen, you'll still find that site.

A Star for the Wildcard

What if you are looking for information on European free trade zones? It is reasonable to assume that Europe free trade zones might also produce good results. Rather than run two searches – European free trade zones and Europe free trade zones – we can use the wildcard notation to match all words that start with Europe (that is, both Europe and European) by typing europe*.

Your Turn

Try the following example:

You Type	It Means
+europe* +"euro"	Find all pages that have words that begin with europe or european or some such. Those same pages must have the word "euro" right next to each other

About how many documents were returned by the query?

Who is Linked to Us?

On the Web, more is better when it comes to site visitors: More visitors means more potential business. Visitors can link to a site in many ways:

1. by deducing or guessing a site name (for example, www.coca-cola.com)
2. by searching for the site using a search engine
3. by copying the address from an advertisement or other media
4. by following a "hot link" from another site

Coopers and Lybrand Consulting found that 39% of Web users learn about sites through other media, 44% through word-of-mouth, 32% through browsing, and 10% through "hot links" (source: www.cyberatlas.com).

We now focus on following a hot link from one site to another and begin with a fun exercise to determine which sites on the Web have a link to our site. The sincerest form of flattery on the Web is to put a free link on a home page to another site. The more folks that do it, the more traffic to the hot-linked site. What if we could find all the sites in the world that have a link to us? Well, we can.

Your Turn

Let's see which sites link to the Board of Governors of the Federal Reserve home page. The address for is www.bog.frb.fed.us. For the first query we want to find all sites that link to the Board of Governors, ordered by the number of times that they mention Board of Governors on their home page.

You Type	It Means
link:www.bog.frb.fed.us	Find all pages with a link to the Board of Governors of the Federal Reserve

How many sites link to the Board of Governors?
Go to the first site on the list. Can you find the link to the Board of Governors? Where was it?

Interestingly, some search engines, but not AltaVista, actually use the number of links to a site to help compute its relevancy ranking. Not a bad idea since the Web community is effectively voting with its links.

Nevertheless, links from other sites are not always welcome. Ticketmaster sued Microsoft for providing a link to its site. The gripe? The Microsoft link did not point to the Ticketmaster home page but rather to a subpage. Ticketmaster wants to communicate with users through the "front door," perhaps so that they will see a full menu of products, promotions, and advertising.

Chapter 3
Getting Your Message Out in Style: E-mail and Other Enhancements

In Chapter 2 we showed you how to conduct searches on the Internet. In other words, you've learned how to get information into your hands from the outside. But as valuable as that skill is, the flow of information has been only one way – to you. How do you move material from your computer to the outside world? Let's turn now to how e-mail works.

Staying in Touch with E-mail

Navigator and most other browsers allow you to communicate through e-mail, newsgroups, and online interest groups. E-mail links are built into many Web pages and enable you to send correspondence directly to other people through the Internet.

E-mail is the electronic exchange of mail. Like Web browsers and Web servers, e-mail operates according to a Client-Server model. Think of the server as your mailbox, where messages addressed to you are stored until you pick them up. You use your mail client to retrieve them. Try to remember to pick up your mail, because if you overload your mailbox, you may lose some pieces.

Getting to an e-mail server is easy. If you are at a campus that has provided you with Internet access, you should be able to apply for an e-mail account through your campus computer administration. Otherwise, you can apply for an e-mail account through an ISP. If you use an ISP to access the Internet, you probably have e-mail capabilities. To properly configure your browser for sending e-mail, you need to know your e-mail address and the name of your mail server.

Here's a little bit on why e-mail addresses look the way they do. The format of a typical e-mail address is as follows: NAME@HOST.DOMAIN. It is not necessary to have a full name for the NAME part of the address. In fact, some addresses use only numbers to represent an individual.

> Here is an example of a typical e-mail address.
>
> joan_waxman@prenhall.com
>
> A typical e-mail address has three basic components:
>
> | | |
> |---|---|
> | user name | joan waxman |
> | host server | prenhall |
> | domain | com |

The @ symbol always follows the user name. The host server appears next. The domain in the e-mail format, just like the domain of the URL format, indicates the user's affiliation. Notice that there are no spaces anywhere in an e-mail address.

Your campus computer administrator or your ISP will provide you with an e-mail account. This is the address you'll give to your friends and perhaps use as part of distance-learning classes. It will also be posted with any correspondence you send on the Internet.

To send and receive e-mail, you need to enter your e-mail address. Once again, in Netscape, move from *Edit* to *References*. Now move to *Mail & Groups*. You'll see the label *Identity*. Click here and fill in the necessary information (Figure 3.1).

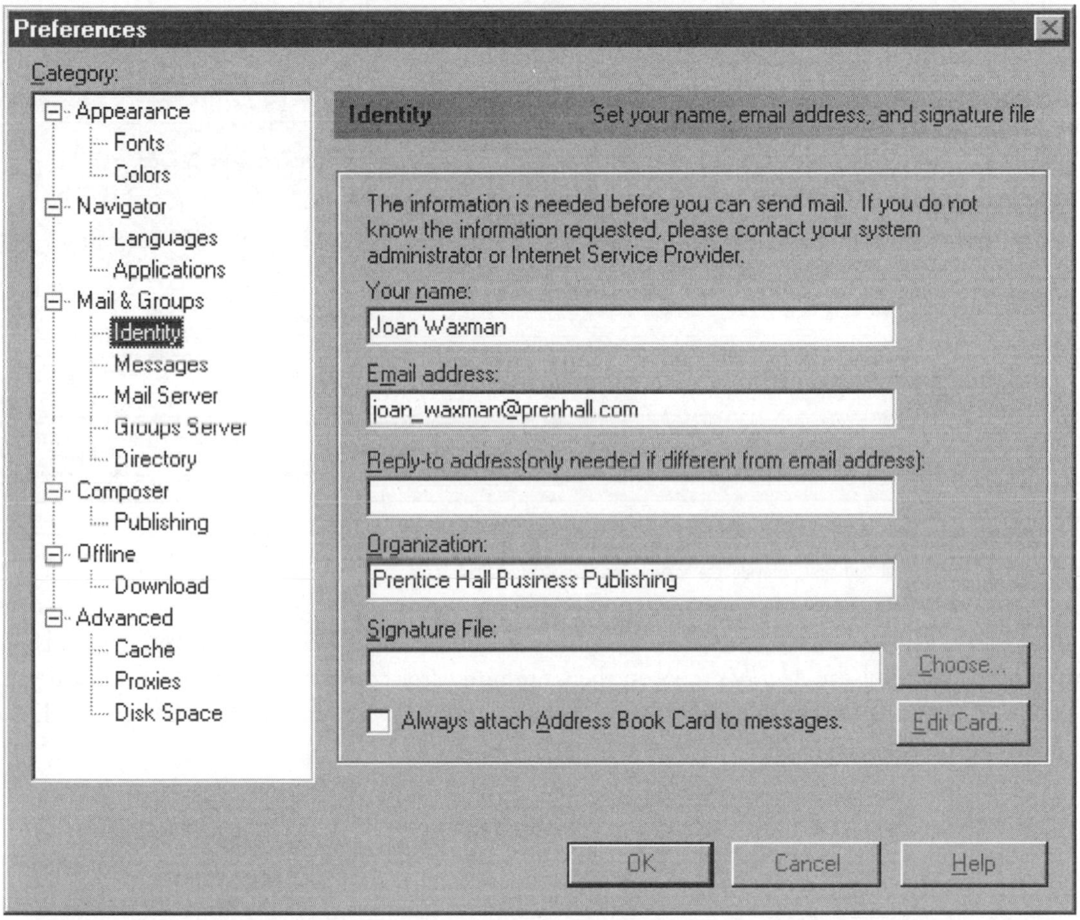

Figure 3.1. You identify yourself for e-mail communication at the Identity section within Preferences.

You need to set up your mail server. Under *Mail & Groups*, simply click on *Mail Server*. Note the directions above the boxes that you must fill in (see Figure 3.2). As they suggest, check with your system administrator or your ISP for the information that you need to enter on this screen.

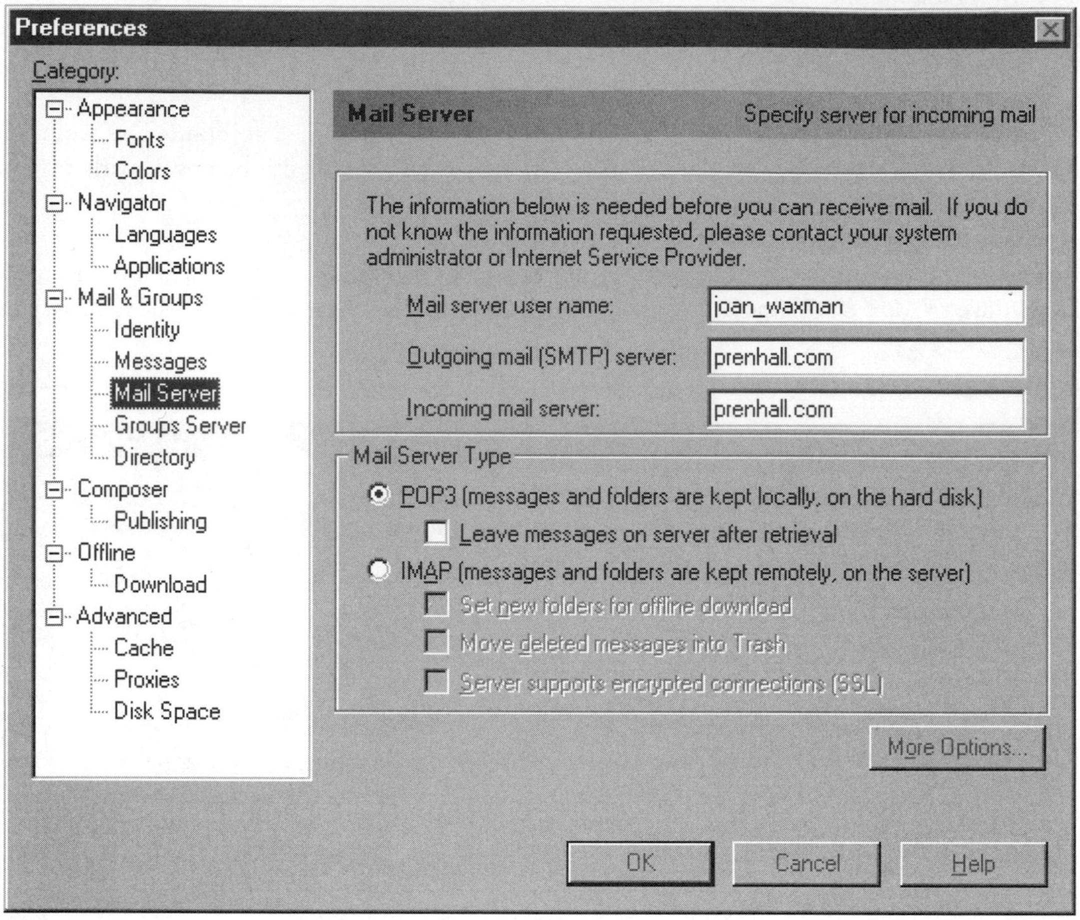

Figure 3.2 Before you can receive mail you must provide the information requested in Mail Server.

Now select the *Communicator* option from the menu bar and choose *Messenger Mailbox.* You could also open your mailbox simply by clicking on the *Mailbox* icon on the Communicator component bar, which is located in the lower right corner of your Netscape Communicator screen or in a floating box somewhere on your screen. Either way you will get a screen that looks like this:

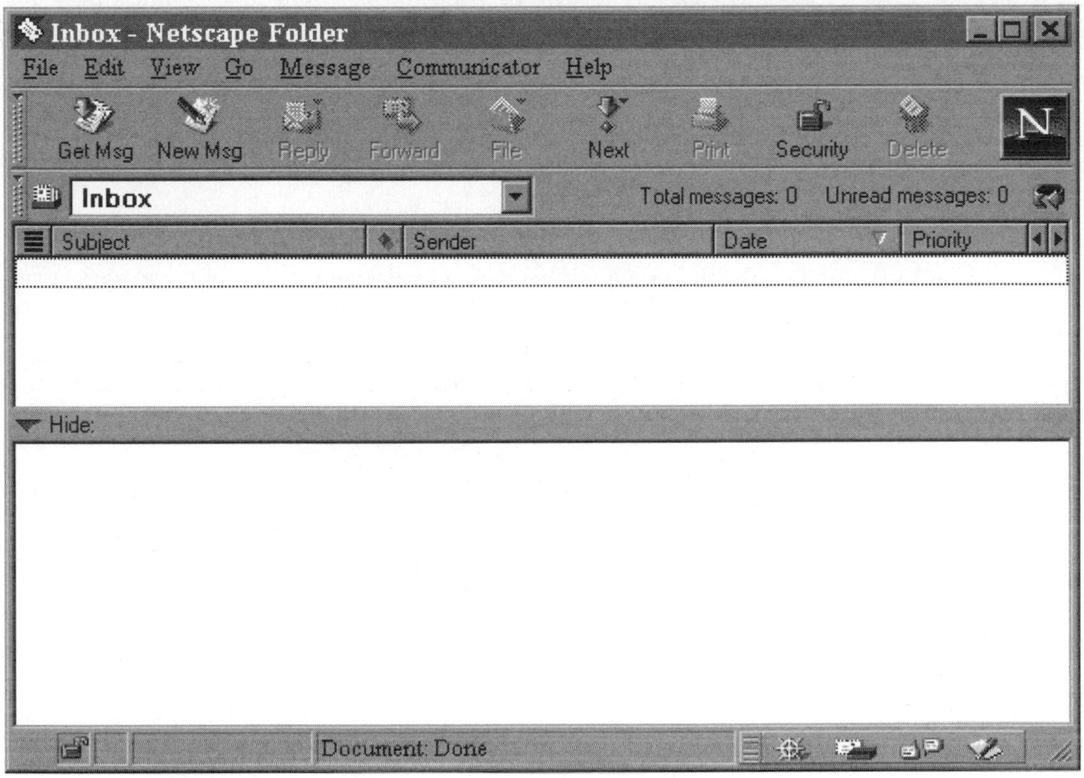

Figure 3.3 The toolbar makes it easy to quickly browse and reply to messages.

To retrieve your mail, select the *Get Msg* button. If you have mail, then it will appear below the *Locator Toolbar*. When you select a specific mail item you will see the contents displayed in the bottom section of the window.

Maybe you know some people with an e-mail address. To send them a note click on the New Msg icon and a new window appears titled Composition. Here is where you will compose and edit the e-mail you send out.

Now that you've got the basics down, here is a site that provides more information on e-mail. It was written by Kaitlin Duck Sherwood.

> A Beginner's Guide to Effective Email
> http://www.webfoot.com/advice/estyle.html?Author

Newsgroups

Many browsers enable users to exchange ideas through newsgroups. A newsgroup is a set of people who connect to an address and participate in a specialized discussion. In some newsgroups, moderators post items for discussion and referee any electronic brawls that may arise. Others function without a moderator. All newsgroups provide a place where people can bring new ideas and perspectives to the table.

Where e-mail is sent and posted for a single person to read, news postings are sent to a common place for all participants to read and comment on. If e-mail is like the postal service, newsgroups are like coffee houses on open microphone night.

What is the purpose of the newsgroups if people just contribute ideas and comments to a mass discussion on a particular topic? Newsgroups are places where you can go and ask questions, get ideas, and learn about specific topics. Select a group that interests you, and see what you find.

The names of newsgroups usually describe their focus. There are several major newsgroup categories. Try the following.

> Here is a typical newsgroup address. Newsgroup names are divided into several descriptive words separated by a period and organized according to a hierarchy. Note that newsgroup addresses don't use the double slash (//).
>
> news:sci.econ.research
>
> Here are the three components, plus the protocol:
>
> | | |
> |---|---|
> | protocol | news: |
> | top category | sci |
> | sub category | econ |
> | sub category | research |

To configure your browser to connect to a newsgroup, you will need the name of the server computer that handles newsgroups. (Get this from the same people who gave you your e-mail server address or search for "public news server" to find one that is available to the general public – there are several.) To set your newsgroup information, select the *Edit* menu and then *Preferences* from the pull-down menu. Select *Groups Server* from the *Mail & Groups* category (see Figure 3.4).

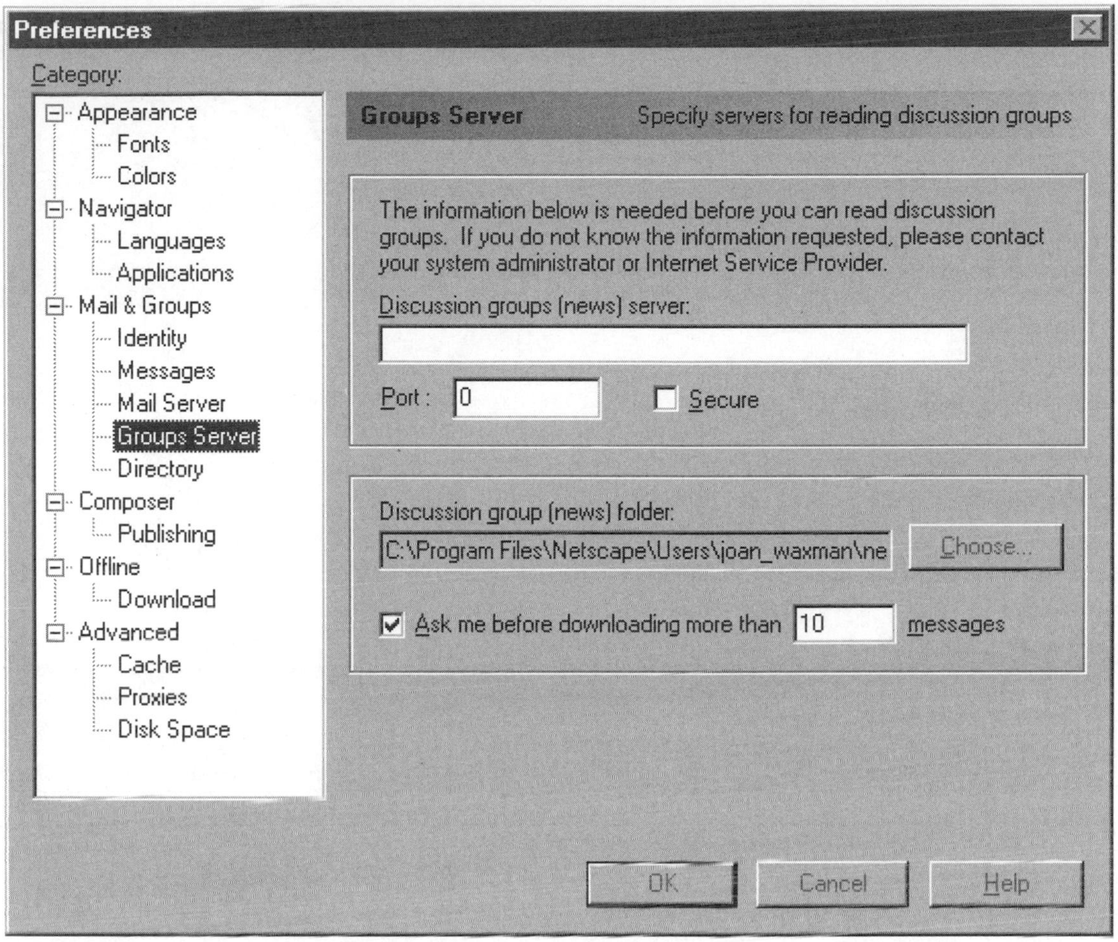

Figure 3.4 Setting preferences in the Mail & Groups category allows you access to e-mail and newsgroups on the Internet.

You may also click on *Collabra Discussion Groups* from the *Communicator* menu, at which point you will be prompted to enter server information. You may find that you can't access some newsgroups. Check to make sure your ISP subscribes to these. If not, it will usually do so if you make a request.

To view a list of newsgroups you can select *Subscribe* from the toolbar and choose *All Groups*. If this is your first time searching for groups, choose *New Groups*. In the future you can update the list in *All Groups* by selecting *New Groups* and clicking on *Get New*. You can subscribe to specific groups by checking them off. Click *OK* when you are finished making your selections. You will then see the selected groups listed in the *Netscape Message Center* window (see Figure 3.5). Finally, when you select a specific article, you will see the contents displayed in the news reader window.

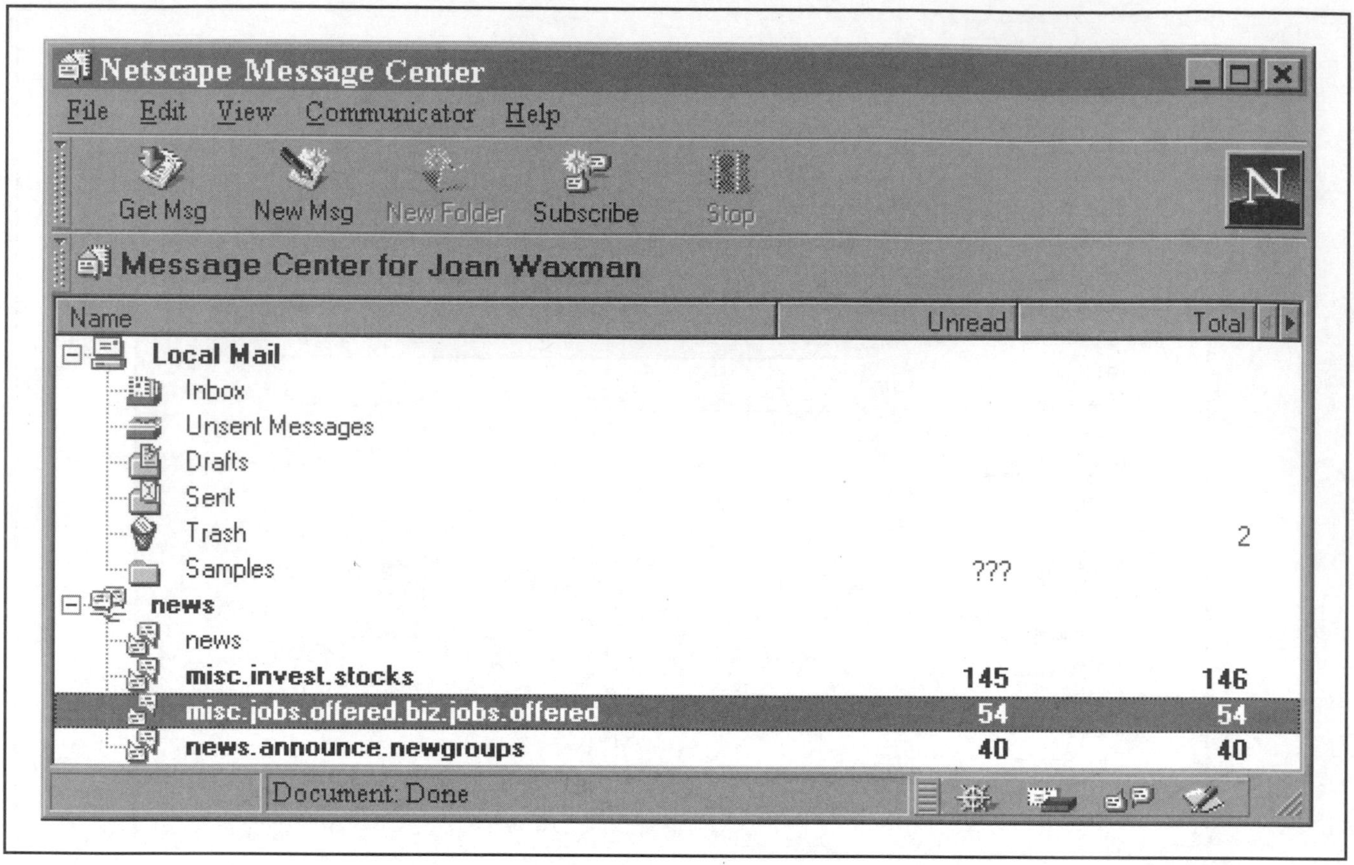

Figure 3.5 Netscape Message Center lists each group you subscribe to. Just click on a newsgroup to view the list of messages.

Chat

This is yet another avenue for communication. It is probably the one you'll choose if you like to gab. Unlike e-mail and newsgroups, which require you to wait for a response, chat rooms are real-time. This means that you are conversing and observing conversations as they happen. Chat rooms are easily accessible through search engines, such as Yahoo! and Excite, and do not require any special browser configuration. As with newsgroups, it is best to observe the interactions of several chat rooms and read the new-user information before you jump in. Some rooms can be excessive and vulgar, but many are frequented by polite people with a genuine desire to communicate honestly. Just like newsgroups, chat rooms are organized by topic, and you can usually anticipate the conversation by the name of the group.

Just to get you started, here are a few Web-based chat groups.

Economics Live Chat
http://mobydicks.com/commons/Economicshall/live/chat.cgi

WWSEconomics
http://www.talkcity.com/chat.htmpl?room=WWSEconomics

Chat - Economics (from The Mining Company, an extremely useful site)
http://economics.miningco.com/mpchat.htm (or go to economics.miningco.com/ and follow the link to chat

Adam Smith Campfire Chat
http://killdevilhill.com/adamsmithchat/live/chat.cgi

Read the instructions and ask for help if you get confused.

Unlike e-mail and newsgroups, you will be frequently asked to log-in or register before you can chat. Often you'll even be given a password. Always read the rules for participating and ask for help if you don't understand something. The participants are generally helpful. In chat rooms you will typically use a "handle," or pseudonym, when you post a message. Some people find chat rooms to be more entertaining than educational, but decide for yourself.

You might also consider communicating through a message board. Quite simply, one person posts a message and other people may reply. The person posting the message and any person responding to it do not have to be logged on at the same time. And all communication is open to any visitor.

To get you started, here are some Web-based message boards related to economics.

Economics Bulletin Board from The Mining Company
http://economics.miningco.com/mpboards.htm

Adam Smith Campfire Chat – Message Board
http://www.killdevilhill.com/adamsmithchat/wwwboard.html

Language for the Road

A few words of caution. Unlike face-to-face conversations between people, electronic exchanges restrict your ability to use vocal inflections, facial expression, and body language while communicating. (These options aren't easily digitized and transmitted across the wires unless you have an Internet telephone or video conference capability. These are available if you have a powerful system, but for most of us they are not practical.) You will need to practice the way you communicate electronically and be patient when someone misinterprets something you've "said." For example, suppose you tell a joke. Because the reader gets only the text, she may think that you are serious and take offense. Computer hacks learned about this problem a long time ago and developed several solutions. They are called smileys. You'll have to turn your head side-ways to view them:

:-)	This is a happy face
;-)	This is a wink
:-(	This is a sad face
:-[	This is a really sad face

Because you eventually will get tired of typing all of the things you want to say, several sets of initials are commonly used. Here are but a few:

BTW	By The Way
IMHO	In My Humble Opinion
FYI	For Your Information
FAQ	Frequently Asked Question

Like any other culture, the Internet has borrowed some common words, but uses them in a context you might not normally expect. Here are two that you'll commonly see:

Flame The act of yelling, insulting, or degrading a person. You can expect to get flamed if you don't follow certain basic rules of netiquette (etiquette of the Net).

Spam The act of posting a comment, message, or advertisement to multiple newsgroups when the note doesn't pertain to them all. It is the Internet equivalent of sending junk mail.

> These are a few Web resources that you will definitely want to read when you begin communicating online. They are very helpful and at times even pretty funny. Enjoy!
>
> E-Mail Etiquette
> http://www.iwillfollow.com/email.htm
> The Net: User Guidelines and Netiquette By Arlene H. Rinaldi
> http://rs6000.adm.fau.edu/rinaldi/net/index.htm
> Electronic Frontier Foundation's Unofficial Smiley Dictionary
> http://www.eff.org/papers/eegtti/eeg_286.html

There's Always Room to Improve

In early Web history, travel was pretty basic. The browser was a piece of software that acted as a totally self-contained vehicle. When you hooked it up, it contained everything you needed to cruise the Net. But as the Web has grown, people have developed new formats for presenting information on the Web. Digital video, audio, animation, interactive games, and 3D worlds are very common on the Internet. Eventually, as people demand more functionality from the Internet, new and richer formats will be developed. To cope with this continuing change, Netscape has developed a way to add functionality without overloading the basic browser design.

Helpers and Plug-ins

Early Web pages included only text and images. They were much like brochures with the ability to hyperlink to other pages. As Web pages grew more sophisticated, so did the format in which their images were presented. The browser was no longer enough to display these images. People had to turn to an external program – that is, a program outside the browser – to display these images. Such an outside program is called a helper application. Some developers decided to eliminate the helper application by bringing it inside the browser software. The result is called a plug-in. A plug-in is any program added to the internal workings of a browser. For example, if you want to listen to music on the Internet, you can install a plug-in that allows the browser to understand the audio format.

Netscape was critical to the development of many plug-ins, and this company is still the place to turn when you want one. An important point: Adding plug-ins to your browser will increase its requirement for memory (RAM). If you go overboard with the plug-ins, your browser might stop working. Add only the plug-ins that you're going to use regularly.

> These addresses will take you to the place where you can download the plug-ins to your computer. These developers also provide a very good description of how to install them and make them work for you.
>
> RealAudio by Progressive Networks
> http://get.real.com/products/player/download.html
>
> Shockwave by MacroMedia
> http://www.macromedia.com/shockwave/download/
>
> QuickTime by Apple
> http://www.quickTime.apple.com/sw/

Once you've lived a little and added a plug-in or two (or too many), you can get a list of the ones you've installed right from your browser. Select the *Help* menu and then choose *About Plug-ins.* The browser window will then present a list of all of your installed plug-ins. If you click on the link at the top of the page, you will also be able to connect directly to Netscape's master plug-in page.

JavaScript and Java

As it turned out, helpers and plug-ins weren't enough. Web developers wanted even more – more flexibility, more interactivity, and more control. Enter JavaScript and Java, two programming languages, to provide the "more" that developers needed.

Web pages communicate ideas by bringing together different media. One type of media, interactive programs, did not exist on the Web until JavaScript and Java became available. People who write programs that do things on Web pages use these programming languages. They add functionality to Web pages, just as helpers and plug-ins do, but they provide much greater flexibility. JavaScript is usually integrated with the Web page and runs on the client side. Java is usually integrated on the server side.

An excellent economics site using Java is "oo...Micro!" a site created and maintained by Dr. Joseph Daniels of the Economics Department at the University of Delaware. He developed the site as a teaching and learning tool for an Intermediate Microeconomics course. It is well worth a visit. The address is:

> oo...Micro!
> http://medusa.be.udel.edu/WWW_Sites/oo_Micro.html

Customizing

You know now how to handle some very important aspects of the Internet. Perhaps at this point you want to fine-tune your set-up. Want to change your home page? Want to change the typeface your screen shows? Let's look at a few options.

Home Page

You might want to modify the location of your home page, which is the screen that appears every time you start up your browser. If you're working with a browser that hasn't been customized before, the company that made the browser probably chose the home page. If you're working on one of your school's computers, then the home page may already be set to the school's page. Find out if you are permitted to change the home page in your computer lab. If it's okay to do so, then decide what you want to set as your home page. By now you've probably found something on the Web that you would want to call home. When your home page is properly set, every time you start your browser or select home from the toolbar, you'll end up at this place, so choose wisely. (However, you can always change your home page again if you want to.)

In Netscape, click on the *Edit* menu and then *Preferences*. If you next highlight *Navigator*, you should get the page that appears in Figure 3.6. Type in the address of whatever you want for your home page in the Location box.

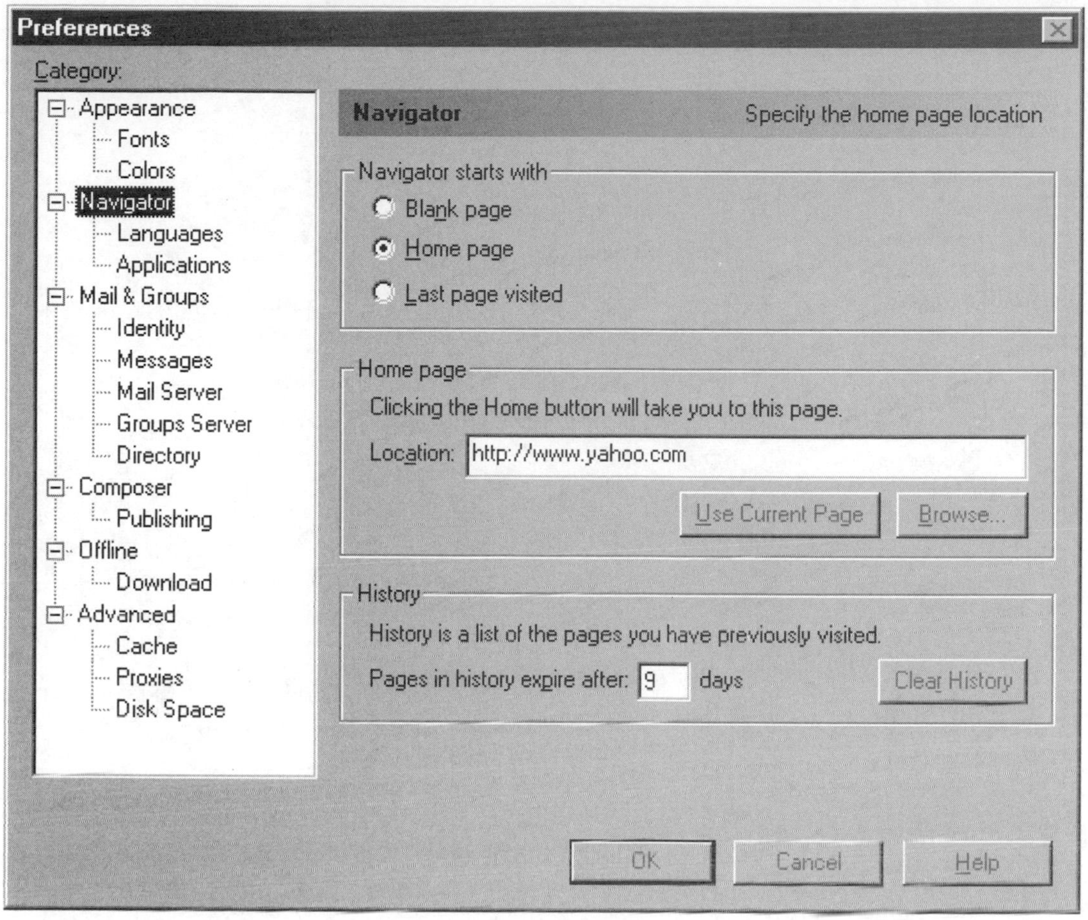

Figure 3.6. Navigator lets you set your home page to any screen you'd like. Just type in the appropriate address. This browser is set to call Yahoo! home.

Setting Options

On the Internet, as in life, *time is money*. Saving time is important if you have to use a modem and an Internet service provider (ISP) to cruise the Net. One way to speed up your Internet travels is to change the *Automatically Load Images* option. The images that appear on the Net's pages make it an attractive place to visit, but loading these images takes time. You might, then, want to turn this option off. Click on *Edit* on the toolbar and select *Preferences*. Now move to *Advanced* (see Figure 3.7). The check-mark in the box means that the images will load. If you click in the box to eliminate the check-mark, Web pages will appear on your screen without the time-consuming images. Try it to see how much more quickly pages load. If you want to restore the *Automatically Load Images* function, just click in the box one more time. The check-mark will reappear, signaling that your browser will again load the Web's images.

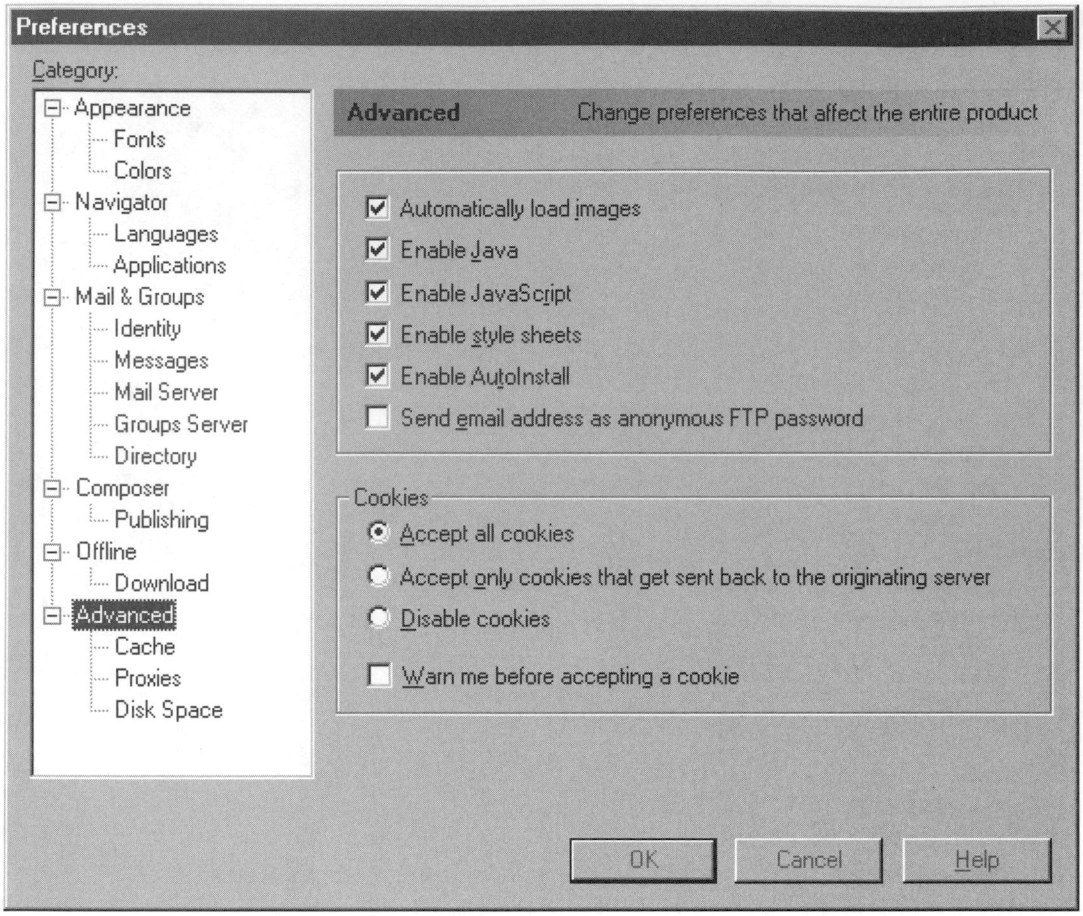

Figure 3.7. Netscape allows you to set many options, among them whether or not images automatically load onto your screen. A check-mark indicates that images will appear.

Other Options

Go to the top bar of Navigator and click on *View*. Note the options that appear. For example, if you want to eliminate the personal toolbar, simply click on *Hide personal toolbar*. To restore it, pull down the *View* menu again and click on *Show personal toolbar*.

Clicking on the word *Edit* at the top of the toolbar lets you set still other options. After pulling down the *Edit* menu, click on *Preferences*. Note the range of options you can set, including font and colors.

Although we have not discussed all of the options, you have enough experience now to explore. Experiment with the settings on your own. However, you do need to be careful. Some options won't apply to your setup. With other options, you will need specific information to ensure that they will work properly with your ISP.

Whatever your question – about setting options or about some other aspect of Netscape – you'll be pleased to know that Netscape provides a wide range of help topics. Just click on the word *Help* at the top of the toolbar. From the sub-menu that appears, choose the top item, *Help Contents*. If you are using Microsoft's Internet Explorer or another browser, you will find that they have very similar features.

Creating Your Traveling Home Page

Earlier we mentioned that you will likely be using the Web from a computer lab somewhere on campus. While that beats having to pay for ISP services, it does have its drawbacks. Perhaps most bothersome is that none of the customization we've discussed and none of the saving techniques, such as bookmarking, will work in a lab. You are probably not going to be working from the same computer next trip and, even if you were, labs tend to have their machines "cleaned" regularly. Nothing you save to a lab drive will be there when you come back, unless you come back quickly.

To get around this situation have a set of links and bookmarks you can carry around on disk. Then just put the disk in the lab computer, load your home page off the disk, and start up, with all your links and bookmarks in place. Unfortunately, any customization you have done, such as setting Netscape to run e-mail or discussion and news groups, cannot be carried from machine to machine quite so easily.

Having your favorite locations stored in a bookmark file and loading that file each session is an adequate way of working on the Web from a computer lab on campus. Eventually, however, you will want to put your own information out on the Internet for others to see. Perhaps you will want to make your bookmark file available for others in your class or study group to use, or you may want to create a Web page with your résumé on it for prospective employers to see. So how do you get your information on the Internet? In the next sections we will be creating an HTML document, referring throughout to the code that appears in the following box, which we'll call the Traveling Home Page.

```
<HTML>
<HEAD>
<TITLE>My Traveling HomePage </TITLE>
</HEAD>

<BODY>

<CENTER>
<H1>Your Name</H1>
<H2>This is my Traveling HomePage</H2>
<H3>If you have found this disk, please return it to<BR>
What should they do? – call you? leave it somewhere? You decide</H3>
</CENTER>

<HR>

<H2>Some Links:</H2>
<H3>Directories and Search Engines:</H3>
<A HREF="http://www.altavista.digital.com/">AltaVista Search Engine</A><BR>
<A HREF="http://www.yahoo.com/">Yahoo Directory</A><BR>
<A HREF="http://www.metacrawler.com/">MetaCrawler Search Engine;</A>

<HR size=4 width="50%" align=left>

<H3>Some Economics Links:</H3>
<A HREF="http://www.economist.com/">The Economist</A><BR>
<A HREF="http://econwpa.wustl.edu/EconFAQ/EconFAQ.html">Resources for Economists on the
Internet</A>

<HR size=4 width="50%" align=left>

<A HREF="bookmark.htm">Show Me My Bookmarks</A>

</BODY>
</HTML>
```

Understanding Your Home Page File

Before we go any further, let's look at the structure of the Traveling Home Page. If you understand how it works, you will find it easier to manage. The language this file is written in is called HyperText Markup Language, or HTML. HTML *commands* are included in brackets < > and tell your browser *how* to display the information.

What about the file itself? There are three fundamental parts to any HTML file. First there is the <HTML> command at the top of the file. This lets your computer know that what follows is written in HTML. Then there is a section called the Header, indicated by the command <HEAD>. The third part is the body of the file itself, indicated by the command <BODY>. In HTML talk, these commands are called *tags*. If you look at the file carefully, you will notice that these tags, and several others, are paired with another similar tag. For example the <HEAD> tag is paired with the </HEAD> tag (note the slash right after the first bracket). This is the basic structure of any markup language. First you tell the computer to begin an action, then you tell it to stop.

Basic HTML Tags

The <HTML> </HTML> tags must be the first and last lines of the file. They "bookend" the entire HTML file. Within the <HEAD> </HEAD> section you can place several things. The most important is the title of the document. The largest section is the <BODY> </BODY> portion. This is where you put the main part of your page.

The best way to learn what these tags do is to look at the "source" file, such as the one we have provided for the Traveling Home Page, and see how the information within different sections of the file actually appears in the Netscape browser. (You can view the source file of any Web page by clicking on the View menu button and then selecting *Document Source* from the menu.) By editing the source file and seeing how the formatting changes on the browser screen, you can quickly learn the basics of HTML authoring. The browser view of the beginning of the Traveling Home Page appears in Figure 3.8.

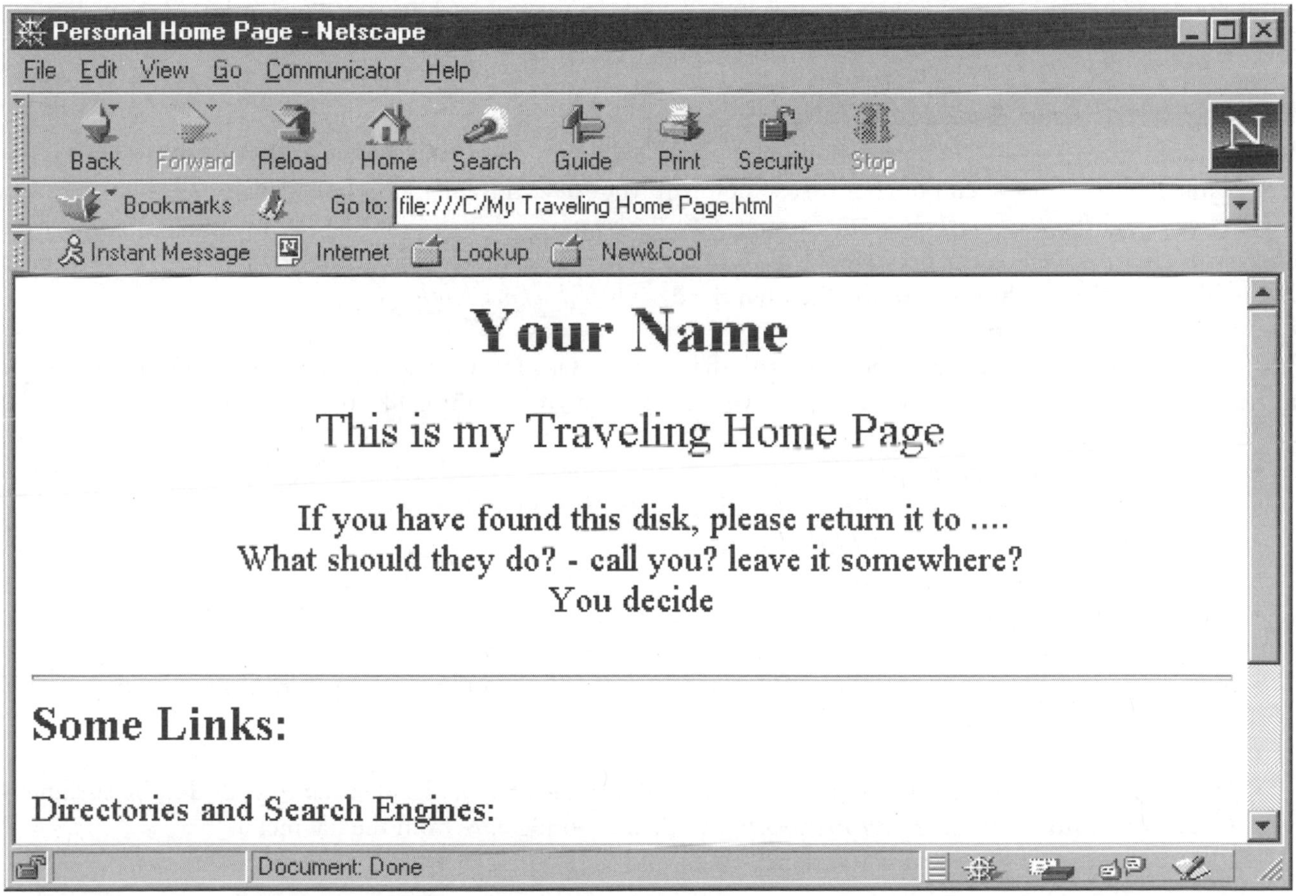

Figure 3.8. This is what the beginning of the Traveling Home Page looks like in Netscape. Compare this to the source file — the code — to determine how the HTML tags work.

Creating and Editing Your Home Page

Now let's actually create the file itself. You can use any word processor or text editor to edit your home page source file. (We have found Notepad from the MS Office Suite to be an excellent HTML-writer. It is clean and simple. You just have to be careful to keep it from adding a .txt extension to your file.) Simply open your text editor and type in the Traveling Home Page code. The parts in *italics* are discretionary –– that is, you can set them to whatever you wish to personalize the file. Then save the file as a *text file or DOS text file* (any ASCII file is fine) to a floppy-disk and name it whatever you wish, as long as it has an htm or html extension. We named ours thp.htm for Traveling Home Page. Treat it just as you would any other text document.

Customizing your Traveling Home Page

Fortunately, you don't have to learn a great deal of HTML code to work with Web pages. Built into Netscape Communicator (and into Netscape Navigator 3.0 and higher) is a pretty good HTML processor. This is much like a word processor except that it creates documents for the Web rather than for a printer. Try it out. Load your Traveling Home Page into Netscape and select Edit Page from the File menu.

Once you have your home page in Composer you may edit it any way you wish. The toolbar is fairly clear and the help is good. Work with your file as much as you wish, and then save it back to your floppy. Just remember, the bigger your Traveling Home Page, the less space you have on the disk for your bookmarks.

Working with Your Bookmark File

One of the main objects of creating the Traveling Home Page file in the first place was to have access to your bookmarks while in a lab. At the end of your first session with your new Traveling Home Page, save your bookmarks by simply clicking on the *Bookmarks* button, selecting *Edit Bookmarks*, and then from the *File* menu selecting *Save As*. When your choice screen comes up, save the file on your floppy disk, which contains your Traveling Home Page file. Be careful not to change the name of the file from the default of *bookmark.htm.*

Now you are set. You have a home page on a disk that you can take from lab to lab. You have your bookmark file on the same disk. So a session with Netscape in your lab should go something like this:

- Come in and start up Netscape
- Put your Traveling Home Page disk in the drive
- Click on *Bookmarks* and select *Edit Bookmarks*
- From the file menu select *Open Bookmark File*
- Choose the bookmark file from your disk and select *Open*
  (You now have your bookmarks available to you when you are browsing)
- Now open your THP file by choosing *Open Page* from the file menu or pressing *Ctrl-O* and selecting it via the *Choose File* button
- You are all set to surf!!
- Once done, if you added any bookmarks you should save the bookmarks file back to your disk by clicking the *Bookmarks* button, choosing *Edit Bookmarks* and then choosing *Save* from the file menu.
- Close down the machine and you're done!

Moving On

Now that you have created your personal home page, experiment with putting links to other Web sites on it. Before too long you will have not just a home page but a personal Web site, and it will be time for you to learn how to upload your site to a server and join the world of Internet content providers! But that's a lesson for another day.

Chapter 4
Sources of Economic Information on the Internet

Like the Internet, economics is everywhere. Each day we are bombarded with news stories that focus on economic topics: downsizing, unemployment, foreign currency crises, free trade, economic development, inflation, mergers, antitrust cases, and hundreds of other economic events and issues affecting individuals, businesses, and governments around the world. How can we make sense out of all this information? Both economic theory and the Internet can help, and when used together, they are powerful tools for understanding how economic events shape our world.

Economic Information and Knowledge

The Internet is widely used for information in economics. It provides a wealth of current and historical data, laws and regulations, news stories, press releases, economic commentaries and analyses, economic forecasts, and general background information that help us understand what is going on in the world.

In this chapter we'll help you find information on the Web that we think is useful for students in a wide variety of economics courses. When compiling this list we avoided the temptation to be encyclopedic. Rather, we have selected Web resources that we have found to be useful in our own classes. The result is a list of economics resources that will provide you with a rich range of information without overwhelming you. Of course, you may find additional Web sites not listed here that are particularly useful to you. In that case, be sure to create a bookmark file so that you can return to them quickly in the future.

The real benefit of the Internet is in helping you better understand the economic concepts in your courses. It is important to remember that while the Internet is a wonderful provider of economic *information*, it is simply a tool in developing economic *knowledge*. To learn economics requires *doing* economics – that is, learning economics requires you to *process* the information you obtain on the Internet and relate it to economic concepts in the classroom.

Sources of Economic Information

One of the problems associated with using the Internet is knowing where to look for information. In this section we'll point you to specific sources of economic information, ranging from broad directories of economic topics to sites containing the latest releases of specific economic statistics. Of course, you could have found much of this same information by using the appropriate keyword in an Internet search engine, but we've tried to organize the information in categories that make it easy to quickly find the information you want. Within each category, in addition to listing the Web site address, we have included a brief summary of the type of information you are likely to find at these sites.

In general, we have focused on sites that provide at least a portion of their information free of charge. Some sites may require you to fill out a free registration, however, to access material.

A Warning: Remember that the Web is a dynamic place. Web site addresses change and sometimes disappear altogether, while new Web sites that offer alternative sources of economic information appear on the scene. In the pages that follow we have tried to select Web sites that we believe will be maintained and updated for at least the next year. In any case, the Web addresses listed here were accurate when this guide was written. If you find that a listed Web site is no longer available, use a search engine to look for the site's new address or sites that contain similar information.

General Indexes and Directories of Economic Information

There are a number of comprehensive directories or indexes of economic information available on the Internet. However, Bill Goffe's *Resources for Economists on the Internet* is the most comprehensive source and is updated regularly. Goffe's *Resources for Economists* is annotated, so in addition to addresses of specific sites there are also brief descriptions of what you can expect to find there. Note that Goffe's guide is also "mirrored" at a number of sites on the Web, but be aware that not all are updated regularly. A recent version of *Resources for Economists on the Internet* can be found at the two sites listed below, which are located at Washington University in St. Louis.

http://wueconb.wustl.edu/EconFAQ/EconFAQ.html
http://econwpa.wustl.edu/EconFAQ/EconFAQ.html

Another useful general-purpose source of current information on economics-related research, learning resources, data, and news topics is the *Scout Report on Business and Economics*, created and distributed by the University of Wisconsin. The *Scout Report* is published biweekly and contains announcements (and brief descriptions) of recent economic data releases, information about recently published research, working papers, and newsletters. It also offers a special focus on a new economic topic in the news each issue. The *Scout Report* can be found at this site:

http://scout.cs.wisc.edu/scout/report/bus-econ/current/index.html

ECONlinks is a less extensive directory of economics links that are particularly applicable to students enrolled in undergraduate economics courses. The *ECONlinks* site was developed by Scott Simkins, one of the authors of this Internet guide, to provide easy student access to important economic and financial information on the World Wide Web. The list of links, which are annotated, focuses on economic topics and concepts that are likely to be encountered in a variety of undergraduate economics courses. The *ECONlinks* site is located at

http://www.ncat.edu/~simkinss/econlinks.html

There are a number of Internet directories that provide broad coverage of economics and business information. These tend to be encyclopedic but often include a search engine to help you narrow the focus of your search. A representative sample follows.

Economics Resources (Rutgers University)
http://www.libraries.rutgers.edu/rulib/socsci/econ/econ.html

YAHOO - Economics
http://www.yahoo.com/Social_Science/Economics/

The Scout Report-Business and Economics: Current Awareness Metapage
http://scout.cs.wisc.edu/scout/report/bus-econ/metapage/

Infoseek - Economics
http://www.infoseek.com/Business/Economics

The Mining Company Guide to Economics
http://economics.miningco.com/

Economics and Finance-related Indexes

The following indexes provide a comprehensive source of economics and finance-related information. These sites focus more closely on information related to stocks, bonds, and financial markets.

FinWeb
http://www.finweb.com/

KiwiClub Web
http://kiwiclub.bus.utexas.edu/

Current National and International News

Read late-breaking news releases on a full range of topics by visiting the following news sites. Content on these sites is continually updated, so stop back often for the latest news and information. In some cases the sites contain links to live *audio* programming and *video* clips of news stories as well as the written text. Many of the sites have specific sections devoted to economic and financial news, as well as weather, sports, travel, and commentaries.

National Newspapers

The New York Times on the Web
http://www.nytimes.com/

The Washington Post
http://www.washingtonpost.com

The Los Angeles Times
http://www.latimes.com

USAToday
http://www.usatoday.com/

The NANDO Times
http://www.nando.net/

Other News Media

CNN Interactive
http://www.cnn.com/

MSNBC (includes audio headlines)
http://www.msnbc.com

ABC News
http://www.abcnews.com/

CBS News
http://www.cbs.com/navbar/news.html

Fox News
http://www.foxnews.com/

YAHOO! News Headlines
http://dailynews.yahoo.com/headlines/

Time Daily
http://cgi.pathfinder.com/time/daily/

Online U.S. News
http://www.usnews.com/usnews/home.htm

National Public Radio
http://www.npr.org

Directories of International Newspapers

Now you can access many of the world's newspapers without leaving your computer! Whether you're investigating economic conditions in Asia or just curious about the world's events from a non-American perspective, the international news directories listed below will help keep you informed.

YAHOO's List of International Newspapers
http://www.yahoo.com/News/Newspapers/Regional/Countries/

International Newspapers (Duke University Library)
http://www.lib.duke.edu/fsb/news.htm

International Newspapers List (University of Oregon)
http://libweb.uoregon.edu/network/enewspap.html

Newspapers On Line
http://www.inesmedia.com/Cgi-bin/ines-geosites.cgi

Electric Book
http://www.electricbook.com/intnews.html

International Newspapers
http://www.ul.cs.cmu.edu/news/international/

International Wire and News Services
http://www1.trib.com/NEWS/APwire.html

Current National and International Business News

A number of online news providers post business news on the Internet as it unfolds, updating the information throughout the day. Many of these sites also provide links to current financial market conditions such as stock indexes, interest rates, and exchange rates, as well as to industry-specific information. Bring the real world to your economics classroom discussions.

The Wall Street Journal Interactive Edition (fee)
http://wsj.com/

Bloomberg's Business News
http://www.bloomberg.com/

Financial Times
http://www.ft.com/

CNNfn - The Financial Network
http://www.cnnfn.com/

Business Wire (Associated Press Breaking News)
http://www.businesswire.com/

The New York Times on the Web - Business Section
http://www.nytimes.com/yr/mo/day/business/

The Washington Post - Business Section
http://www.washingtonpost.com/wp-srv/business/front.htm

The Los Angeles Times - Business Section
http://www.latimes.com/HOME/BUSINESS/

CNBC Business and Wall Street Journal Highlights
http://www.msnbc.com/news/COM_Front.asp

ABC Business News
http://www.abcnews.com/sections/business/

CBS News (Money)
http://www.cbs.com/navbar/news.html

Fox Marketwire
http://www.foxmarketwire.com/

USAToday Money
http://www.usatoday.com/money/mfront.htm

YAHOO News - Business (Reuters)
http://dailynews.yahoo.com/headlines/business/

Reuters
http://www.reuters.com/

Latest Asian Business News and Markets from Bridge News
http://www.asia-inc.com/knight/

Economic Indicators and Statistics

Check out the news behind the headlines and keep up to date with current economic events. The sites below provide a general overview of recent and current economic conditions, as well as important economic statistics. The reports and statistics are updated regularly, in some cases daily or weekly.

Economic Indicators - General Overview

Dr. Ed Yardeni's Economics Network
http://www.yardeni.com/

The Dismal Scientist
http://www.dismal.com/

Economic Statistics Briefing Room
http://www.whitehouse.gov/fsbr/esbr.html

Bureau of Economic Analysis
http://www.bea.doc.gov/

BLS Economy at a Glance
http://stats.bls.gov:80/eag.table.html

Bureau of Economic Analysis Overview of the Economy
http://www.bea.doc.gov/bea/glance.htm

USA Today Economy Track
http://www.usatoday.com/money/economy/econ0001.htm

The Federal Reserve's Beige Book
http://www.bog.frb.fed.us/FOMC/BeigeBook/default.cfm

The State of the Economy
http://www.dryden.com/state.html

Current Economic Statistics

GDP, Personal Income, International Trade
(Bureau of Economic Analysis News Releases)
http://www.bea.doc.gov/bea/rels.htm

Employment, Prices (Inflation), and Productivity
(Bureau of Labor Statistics News Releases)
http://www.bls.gov/newsrels.htm

Interest Rates (Federal Reserve)
http://www.bog.frb.fed.us/releases/h15/About.HTM
http://www.ny.frb.org/pihome/mktrates/dlyrates/

Exchange Rates (International Monetary Fund and Federal Reserve)
http://www.imf.org/external/np/tre/sdr/drates/8101.htm
http://www.ny.frb.org/pihome/mktrates/forex12.shtml

Current Financial Market Information

These sites provide direct links to current financial market information such as interest rates, exchange rates, stock market indexes, mutual fund indexes, and individual stock and mutual fund quotes. The information is continually updated so you can keep track of financial information throughout the day.

YAHOO Finance
http://quote.yahoo.com/

CBS MarketWatch
http://cbs.marketwatch.com/news/newsroom.htx

CNN Financial Web Pages

U.S. Stock Markets
http://www.cnnfn.com/markets/us_markets.html

Currency Exchange Rates
http://www.cnnfn.com/markets/currencies.html

World Stock Market Indexes
http://www.cnnfn.com/markets/world_markets.html

USA Today Market Scoreboard
http://www.usatoday.com/money/msfront.htm

Bloomberg
http://www.bloomberg.com/welcome.html

Economic Analysis and Forecasts

The two sites listed below contain a wealth of information on current economic conditions as well as economic analyses and forecasts.

Dr. Ed Yardeni's Economics Network
http://www.yardeni.com/

The Dismal Scientist
http://www.dismal.com/

Major banks also provide some of the best information about current economic conditions. If you want to get a summary of what's happening in the U.S. and international economy, as well as a short-term forecast of economic conditions, check out these sites.

Morgan Stanley Global Economic Forum
http://www.ms.com/GEF/index.html

First Union Bank Economic Information
http://www.firstunion.com/econews/
- Weekly Economic Indicator Analysis
- Weekly Economic Commentary
- Weekly International Economic Commentary
- Quarterly Economic Outlook

CITICORP Market Information
http://www.citibank.com/us/investments/market/market.htm
- Market Commentary
- Market Snapshot
- Economic Calendar
- Currency Rates, Stock Quotes, and Stock Market Performance

Wells Fargo Economic Reports
http://wellsfargo.com/econ/
- U.S. Economic Commentary
- Foreign Exchange Report

Bank of America Economic Analysis
http://www.bankamerica.com/econ_indicator/econ_indicator.html
- Weekly U.S. Economic Briefing
- Weekly International Economic Briefing
- U.S. Economic Forecasts
- Exchange Rate Forecasts

U.S. Historical Data

If you have a research project or assignment that requires U.S. economic data, here are a few places to look. Some of the sites provide graphs as well as numbers.

Directories and Sources of National Data

Directories

Social Science Data on the Internet (Univ. of California, San Diego)
http://odwin.ucsd.edu/idata/

Econ Data and Links (Data and Directory)
http://www.csufresno.edu/Economics/econ_EDL.htm

Business and Economics Numeric Data (Directory)
http://www.clark.net/pub/lschank/web/ecostats.html

WebEc Economic Data (Directory)
http://www.helsinki.fi/WebEc/webecc8d.html

Data Sources

Economic Indicators Monthly
http://www.gpo.ucop.edu/catalog/econind.html

Bureau of Labor Statistics
http://stats.bls.gov:80/datahome.htm

Federal Reserve Economic Data
http://www.stls.frb.org/fred/

Census Bureau Statistics
http://www.census.gov/

Statistical Abstract of the U. S.
http://www.census.gov/stat_abstract/

Social Sciences Data Center (U. of Virginia)
National Income and Product Accounts
http://www.lib.virginia.edu/socsci/nipa/nipa.html

NBER MacroHistory Database
http://www.nber.org/databases/macrohistory/contents/index.html

Economic Policy Institute Datazone
http://epinet.org/datazone/deepdata1.htm

USDA Economic Statistics
http://usda.mannlib.cornell.edu/usda/usda.html

Economic Time Series Page
http://bos.business.uab.edu/data/data.htm

Sources of Regional Data

Regional Economic Information Service (U. of Virginia)
http://www.lib.virginia.edu/socsci/reis/

Census Bureau Statistics - Demographic and Economic State and County Profiles
http://www.census.gov/datamap/www/index.html

Bureau of Labor Statistics Regional Information
http://stats.bls.gov:80/regnhome.htm

County and City Databook
http://www.lib.virginia.edu/socsci/ccdb/

International Data

Some of these sites provide country-specific information on social and economic conditions in addition to economic statistics. The references in the *International Economics Resources* and *International Central Banks* sections are also likely sources of international data.

Penn World Tables
http://arcadia.chass.utoronto.ca/pwt/
http://www.nber.org/pwt56.html

CIA World Fact Book
http://www.odci.gov/cia/publications/factbook/index.html

Statistics Canada
http://www.statcan.ca/start.html

EuroStat (Statistical Office of the European Communities)
http://europa.eu.int/en/comm/eurostat/eurostat.html

U.S. Federal Reserve Banks and International Central Banks

The Federal Reserve system is made up of 12 regional Federal Reserve banks and the Board of Governors, which oversees the entire U.S. banking system and carries out U.S. monetary policy. Each Federal Reserve bank, as well as the Board of Governors, maintains a Web site that contains data, information on regional economic conditions, educational material, and historical information.

Many of the regional Federal Reserve banks provide online publications exploring current economic and financial issues, as well as links to summaries of current economic conditions, current and historical economic statistics, and public-information documents relating to money, banking, and financial markets.

Every major industrialized country has its own central bank, which is responsible for overseeing the safety of the banking industry within that country as well as carrying out monetary policy. The following two sites provide an index of many of these central banks. Each contains country-specific information about the economy, the monetary system, and economic policy. In addition, many of these banks are wonderful sources of international economic and financial data.

International Central Banks

YAHOO Central Banks Index
http://www.yahoo.com/Business_and_Economy/Finance_and_Investment/Banking/Central_Banks/

Mark Bernnkopf's Central Banking Resource Center
http://adams.patriot.net/~bernkopf/

U.S. Federal Reserve System

Board of Governors of the Federal Reserve System
http://www.bog.frb.fed.us/

Fed. Res. Bank of Atlanta
http://www.frbatlanta.org/

Fed. Res. Bank of Boston
http://www.bos.frb.org

Fed. Res. Bank of Chicago
http://www.frbchi.org/

Fed. Res. Bank of Cleveland
http://www.clev.frb.org/

Fed. Res. Bank of Dallas
http://www.dallasfed.org/

Fed. Res. Bank of Kansas City
http://www.kc.frb.org/

Fed. Res. Bank of Minneapolis
http://woodrow.mpls.frb.fed.us/

Fed. Res. Bank of New York
http://www.ny.frb.org/

Fed. Res. Bank of Philadelphia
http://www.phil.frb.org

Fed. Res. Bank of Richmond
http://www.rich.frb.org/

Fed. Res. Bank of St. Louis
http://www.stls.frb.org/

Fed. Res. Bank of San Francisco
http://www.frbsf.org/

Economics and Business-related Magazines

Most major business periodicals have a Web version with access to articles from the current issue. These are a great source of current-events articles.

The Economist
http://www.economist.com/

Fortune
http://www.pathfinder.com/fortune/

Business Week
http://www.businessweek.com/

Forbes
http://www.forbes.com/

U.S. Government Agencies and Other Government Sites

U.S. government agencies are the primary providers of most economic and social statistics. You can gain direct access to these agencies using the sites listed below. Many of these agencies publish a broad range of useful government documents online.

Library of Congress-Explore The Internet
http://lcweb.loc.gov/global/explore.html

Government Information Locator
http://info.er.usgs.gov/gils/index.html

THOMAS Legislative Info.
http://thomas.loc.gov/

The White House
http://www.whitehouse.gov/WH/Welcome.html

Office of Management and Budget
http://www.whitehouse.gov/WH/EOP/omb

Department of the Treasury
http://www.ustreas.gov/

Social Security Administration
http://www.ssa.gov/SSA_Home.html

Internal Revenue Service
http://www.irs.ustreas.gov/prod/

Department of Commerce
http://www.doc.gov/

Bureau of Economic Analysis
http://www.bea.doc.gov/

Bureau of Labor Statistics
http://stats.bls.gov/

Census Bureau
http://www.census.gov/

Federal Deposit Insurance Corporation
http://www.fdic.gov/

U.S. Government Publications

Listed below are a number of U.S. government documents that are particularly useful for economics students. For example, the annual *Economic Report of the President* includes in-depth discussions of microeconomic and macroeconomic policy issues as well as an extensive database of U.S. (and some international) macroeconomic information.

U.S. Government Printing Office
http://www.access.gpo.gov/index.html

Government Printing Office Databases (GPO Access)
http://www.access.gpo.gov/su_docs/dbsearch.html
http://www.gpo.ucop.edu/

U.S. Budget Information (1996, 1997, 1998, and 1999 Federal Budgets)
http://www.access.gpo.gov/su_docs/budget/index.html

Economic Report of the President (1995, 1996, 1997, 1998)
http://www.access.gpo.gov/su_docs/budget/index.html
http://www.access.gpo.gov/eop/index.html

U.S. Occupational Outlook Handbook
http://stats.bls.gov/ocohome.htm

North American Free Trade Agreement
http://www.whitehouse.gov/WH/Publications/html/nafta.html

International Economics Resources

There are numerous international economic organizations that make press releases, economic analyses, and public policy discussions available on the Web. If you are looking for international economic information, check out the following sites.

European Union Information
http://europa.eu.int

G7 Information Centre
http://www.g7.utoronto.ca/

International Monetary Fund
http://www.imf.org

Organization for Economic Cooperation and Development
http://www.oecdwash.org/
http://www.oecd.org/

United Nations
http://www.un.org/

World Bank
http://www.worldbank.org/

World Economic Outlook (World Bank)
http://www.imf.org/external/pubs/ft/weo/weo0598/index.htm

World Trade Organization
http://www.wto.org/

Law and Economics Resources

The Internet sites listed below provide a good starting point for investigating the relationship between law and economics. Many of the sites provide extensive links to other law and economics resources.

The Law and Economics Site
http://www.findlaw.com/lawecon/

Antitrust Policy
http://www.antitrust.org/

RISKWeb
http://www.riskweb.com/

SEC Edgar Database
http://www.sec.gov/edgarhp.htm

Labor Economics Resources

The following Web sites provide information on labor unions, workers' rights, wage and salary determination, and a variety of other issues related to working life.

Berkeley's Guide to Labor Oriented Internet Resources
http://www.lib.berkeley.edu/IIRL/iirlnet.html
http://socrates.berkeley.edu/~iir/library/blg.html

AFL-CIO Home Page
http://www.aflcio.org

The Minimum Wage
http://www.dol.gov/dol/esa/public/minwage/main.htm

Economic and Social Policy Institutes

Economic policy institutes conduct research on a variety of economic and social issues. Some institutes have a conservative or liberal focus, while others remain nonpartisan. By analyzing opposing viewpoints of a public policy issue you will gain an appreciation for the power of economic ideas and economic reasoning. Use the resources at these sites to hone your economic skills and to learn to differentiate between logical economic arguments and political rhetoric.

Electronic Policy Network
http://www.epn.org/

American Enterprise Institute
http://www.aei.org/

American Institute for Economic Research
http://www.aier.org/

Brookings Institution
http://www.brook.edu/

Cato Institute
http://www.cato.org/

Economic Policy Institute
http://epinet.org/

The Heritage Foundation
http://www.heritage.org/

Hoover Institution
http://www-hoover.stanford.edu/

Institute for International Economics
http://www.iie.com/

The Jerome Levy Economics Institute
http://www.levy.org/

National Bureau of Economic Research
http://nber.harvard.edu/

National Center for Policy Analysis
http://www.public-policy.org/~ncpa/

Progressive Policy Institute
http://www.dlcppi.org/

RAND
http://www.rand.org/

The Twentieth Century Fund
http://epn.org/tcf/xxecon.html

The Urban Institute
http://www.urban.org/

Information, Tutorials, Demonstrations, and Hands-on Practice of Economics

Economics instructors are increasingly using the Internet to help students learn economics. In some cases, instructors have added Web links to reading material that goes beyond textbook coverage, while in other cases they have constructed online tutorial packages or entire Web-based courses. Use the following economic education links to supplement your in-class learning.

Directories of Educational Resources and Online Economics Courses

EcEdWeb
http://ecedweb.unomaha.edu/

The Mining Company: Online Resources for Economics Teachers
http://economics.miningco.com/library/weekly/aa102197.htm

EconomicsAmerica EconEdLink
http://www.economicsamerica.org/econedlink/index.html

World Lecture Hall-Economics
http://www.utexas.edu/world/lecture/eco/

World Bank Economic Development Institute (Resources for Teachers and Trainers)
http://www.worldbank.org/html/edi/resource.html

The Scout Report - Business and Economics
http://wwwscout.cs.wisc.edu/scout/report/bus-econ/current/index.html

Amos World
http://amos.bus.okstate.edu/

Samples of Online Economics Textbooks and Courses

CyberEconomics (Online textbook)
http://ingrimayne.saintjoe.edu/econ/TitlePage.html

HyperStats Online (Online textbook)
http://www.ruf.rice.edu/~lane/hyperstat/contents.html

Essential Principles of Economics: A Hypermedia Text (Online textbook)
http://william-king.www.drexel.edu/top/prin/txt/EcoToC.html

Understanding the World Macroeconomy (Online Course)
http://www.stern.nyu.edu/~nroubini/MACRO3.HTM

Amos World Reading Room
http://amos.bus.okstate.edu/read/

Using and Practicing Economic Skills

Economics Minute
http://www.economicsamerica.org/econedlink/minute/index.html

oo_Micro!
http://medusa.be.udel.edu/WWW_Sites/oo_Micro.html

Classroom Expernomics
http://www.marietta.edu/~delemeeg/expernom.html

Iowa Electronic Markets
http://www.biz.uiowa.edu/iem/index.html

The Election Calculator
http://www.mit.edu/people/irons/myjava/ecalc.html

The National Budget Simulator
http://garnet.berkeley.edu:3333/budget/budget.html

Currency Converter
http://oanda.com/cgi-bin/ncc?user=worldbus

Improving Math and Graphing Skills

Graph Skills for Introductory Economics
http://syllabus.syr.edu/cid/pretest/indexT.html

Study Tips for Economics Courses
http://www.utexas.edu/student/lsc/handouts/1409.html

Math and Graphing Skills Tutorial for Economics Students
http://syllabus.syr.edu/cid/graph/TOCbook.html

Chapter 5
Turning Economic Information into Economic Knowledge

As we stated at the beginning of the last chapter, while the Internet is a wonderful source of economic *information*, how you use that information will determine how much economic *knowledge* you will ultimately develop. Creating economic knowledge requires you to combine the information available on the Web with the theory in your economics courses. Economic theory provides a framework to organize new information in a meaningful way and to help you analyze, forecast, and make decisions. These are the lifelong learning skills that economics will help you develop, but they require your active participation in the learning process.

In this chapter we have included a number of economic learning activities that requires you to obtain information on the Web and *process that information* to defend an economic argument, illustrate an economic concept, or make an economic decision. Our purpose is to get you to incorporate the vast amount of information available on the Internet into your economics class.

Some of the activities summarized here were originally included as part of Prentice Hall's Web-based *PHLIP* project and many have been tried in our own classrooms. PHLIP stands for Prentice Hall's Learning on the Internet Partnership and is a dynamic Web site supplying up-to-date information on economics and business-related issues to accompany Prentice Hall textbooks. The *PHLIP* Web site features summaries of economic news stories, along with related group activities, research ideas, and discussion questions that accompany text material. The *PHLIP* Web site can be found at

http://www.phlip.marist.edu/

You might suggest one or more of the activities listed in this chapter to your own instructor as a class project.

A Note on Citing Internet Sources

As a student you regularly cite books, journals, magazines, and newspapers in your research projects. When obtaining information from the Internet the same rules apply: You need to cite your online sources of data, information, sounds, graphics, and video clips. Besides being a good general practice, it allows others to quickly find the same information. The following Web sites will help you become familiar with the bibliographic form these citations should take:

Classroom Connect: Citing Internet Resources
http://www.classroom.com/resource/CitingNetResources.html

MLA Citation Guide
http://www.cas.usf.edu/english/walker/mla.html

Launch to Citing Online Addresses
http://www.pitsco.inter.net/p/cite.html

Williams College Library Web
http://www.williams.edu:803/library/library.www/cite.html

The Internet as an Economics Learning Tool: An Example

The following example shows how you might combine the information-gathering tools of the Internet with economic theory to solve a typical business problem.

Your Assignment

Let's say that at the start of the day your boss has called you into her office for an important meeting. She's going to be making a presentation to the company's top executives and needs

(1) a summary of the current state of the national and regional economies,
(2) a six-month forecast of future economic conditions, and
(3) an analysis of how those conditions will affect industry sales

all by tomorrow! The executives are making a strategic business decision: whether to begin production of a major new line of furniture or postpone production until a later date. Making the right decision could increase sales and profits dramatically, or alternately, save the company millions of dollars in inventory warehousing costs.

Planning: Determining the Information You Will Need to Find and How to Use It

You've got a day to put together this summary, but where to begin? The solution to this problem has several steps: (1) gathering information about current economic activity, (2) combining that information with economic theory to forecast future economic conditions, and (3) determining how expected future conditions will affect company sales. The planning stage of the project requires you to ask questions about what information you will need to find, what the relevant economic theory is, and how to combine the information you find with the appropriate economic theory to produce an accurate economic forecast.

Gathering Data

For this project you'll need to find as much information as you can about current and projected economic conditions in your area and in the nation – statistics like retail sales, employment, inflation rates, interest rates, income, and new housing starts. In addition, you'll need to determine what "story" these statistics are telling:

Is the economy in a recession?
Is economic activity slowing or accelerating?
Is inflation a problem?
How is the Federal Reserve likely to respond?
Are interest rates likely to fall or rise during the coming months?

Start your data gathering by looking at Internet sites that present recent economic statistics, as well as the Federal Reserve's *Beige Book*, to get a feel for current regional and national economic conditions. Online magazines such as *Fortune* or *Business Week* often provide additional insights about recent trends in the economy and some banks provide economic analyses and forecasts on the Internet.

Next, use a search engine to find still more information, perhaps using keywords such as "economy," "current economic conditions," "Federal Reserve," and "economic forecasts." This is the data-gathering stage of your task, and this is where the Internet is most useful.

What information can you find about general economic conditions in the nation and in your area?
List some of the sites that you find in the table below:

Web Site	Information Available at this Web Site
http://www.bog.frb.fed.us	Federal Reserve Beige Book; describes economic conditions in each region of the country

Carrying Out the Economic Analysis

After obtaining a broad range of information on economic conditions, you need to analyze this information and concisely summarize your conclusions.

Are the economic statistics you gathered telling a consistent story, or are various economic indicators giving you conflicting information?
Do you need to gather additional data?

Next, you need to determine how the information you obtained relates to economic theory.

If inflation rates are increasing, is it due to expanding consumer demand or a rise in input prices, such as the price of oil?
If the economy is slowing, what is causing the slowdown – a drop in consumer or business purchases?

Understanding the underlying causes of current economic conditions may help you predict important policy responses by the government or the Federal Reserve that could affect your forecast of company sales.

Making an Economic Forecast

Using economic theory to organize your information, construct a forecast of expected future economic conditions, taking into account any policy actions the Federal Reserve or the government might take. You might consider making multiple forecasts, making different assumptions about likely economic scenarios. Next, think about assigning probabilities to each scenario to give your boss a feel for how changing economic conditions could affect important economic variables related to company sales.

Analysis: Determining the Implications for Your Company

What are the implications of these economic forecasts for your industry and company? For example, if the economy seems to be gaining momentum, but inflation is beginning to increase, how is the Federal Reserve likely to react? Is the Federal Reserve likely to raise interest rates or leave them alone? Interest rates play an important role in determining new home sales, and the pace of new home buying is important for the furniture industry. If the Federal Reserve raises interest rates, for example, the resulting slowdown in home sales will likely translate into fewer orders for new furniture.

At this point you're ready to summarize your economic analysis and present it to your boss. If your projections are consistent with economic theory and are supported by the data you have collected, you can be confident that you have made the best forecast possible. It pays to go back over your analysis to make sure you have been thorough – a business decision based on incomplete analysis could have disastrous effects on your company and leave you without a job.

What have you learned?

What does an exercise like this teach you? First, the Internet can significantly reduce the amount of time it takes to gather information. Without the Internet, gathering the required information would be a formidable and time-consuming task. It would require looking in multiple sources – magazines, newspapers, trade publications, government documents – and would most likely involve a trip to the library. Second, the Internet is a learning *tool*, not a substitute for learning.

At this time the Internet functions much like a library, putting an enormous amount of information at your fingertips. Economics is about learning to use that information to analyze, explain, and predict economic behavior. The Internet is a useful tool for gathering information, but making this information useful to your company also involves economic theory. Combining the two helps companies make better business decisions.

Using the Internet to Help You Learn Economics: More Ideas

The exercise in the previous section gave you a feel for putting the Internet to work in your economics course and in your job. In this section we present additional ideas to illustrate how you might use the Internet to deepen and broaden your understanding of economics. In our choice of activities we have chosen to be selective rather than encyclopedic, and in many cases the ideas reflect our own teaching backgrounds. We encourage you to construct your own strategies for using the Internet.

Developing an Economics E-zine

Design and develop a class electronic economics "magazine" on the Web. The magazine could be updated regularly and provide links to economic statistics, written analysis of economic conditions, commentary on economic events, and updates on class projects and assignments. You could relate economic concepts being discussed in class to local or campus news stories or discuss how national economic policy might affect the students or residents in your area. The possibilities are endless - use your imagination and your growing understanding of economics to bring economics to life!

Your Turn

What topics should be included in your online magazine?
Toward the end of the course, evaluate your Web creation. What are the strengths and weaknesses of your site? What changes would you make?
Invite students at other universities to view your site, or, better yet, collaborate with students at another university (across town, in a different state, or even a different country) to create a joint project.

Linking Current Events and Economic Theory

Because information on the Internet can be updated almost continuously, the Internet provides an ever-changing sea of information about current economic and business events. Visit online business news sites, magazines, and newspapers frequently to obtain the latest news and information about the economy, businesses, and financial markets.

Try to link the news stories you find to the theory you are learning in your economics course. Talk to other students about the stories you have read and see if they can provide new economic insights you may have overlooked. Discussing real-world events in the classroom or during informal conversations with friends helps bring economic theory alive and helps you make connections between economic theory and the real world.

Your Turn

What economics/business stories are making headlines today?
How are these stories related to the economic theory that you are learning in your economics course?

Exploring Economic Policy Issues

Analyzing current economic policy issues provides an opportunity to try out your economic skills. *The Economic Report of the President,* as well as articles from *Business Week, Fortune,* and *The Economist* often provide detailed insights on important economic policy issues. You might also try Web sites for economic-policy institutes. Use economic theory and models to analyze the policy arguments you find. How do political considerations affect the economic policy conclusions that the writers come up with?

Your Turn

Find a Web site that contains information about one of the following policy issues (use a search engine), and use economic analysis to determine the validity of any claims that are made.

- Privatizing Social Security
- The Role of Government in the Economy
- The Relationship Between Inflation and Unemployment
- Reducing Trade Barriers
- European Monetary Union

Welfare Reform
Environmental Policy
Antitrust Policy

What other topics can you think of? Look at chapter section headings, examples, and key words in your textbook for additional ideas.
Do an Internet search to see what you can find out about these issues and how they are related to economics.

Economic Debates

Rather than simply analyzing economic policy issues, conduct a class debate. Debate a current issue, focusing on *economic* arguments to back up your claims. For example, you might hold a mock Congressional hearing on the merits of privatizing the Social Security system or eliminating affirmative action programs. The Web provides a wealth of information on a variety of public policy issues. In addition, you might invite outside "experts" (such as professors in business or political science, retired workers, local public officials and business leaders) to participate in or judge the debate.

Your Turn

How do the economic arguments on an issue differ from *political* arguments?
How does an "economic way of thinking" help to structure your arguments for or against an issue?

Analyzing Economic Data

To put your economic thinking skills to work, obtain recent values of the economic variables discussed in the macroeconomics chapters in your text. Use a spreadsheet program such as Excel or Lotus to analyze and graph them. How can you explain the economic behavior you observe? Is it consistent with the theory you are learning?

Your Turn

Look up data on the Consumer Price Index (CPI), and use this information to calculate U.S. inflation rates over the past few years. In addition, obtain unemployment data over the same years.

What relationship do these two variables display?
Do they move together or in opposite directions?
What might account for this behavior?
How can you relate this to economic theory?
How does this behavior compare to that experienced in other countries over the same period?
What might account for the differences?

Computing Stock Market Returns in U.S. and Foreign Markets

Are you better off investing money in the U.S. stock market or a foreign stock market? To provide some perspective on this question, compare the returns you could earn in the U.S. stock market (using the Dow Jones Industrial Average index) with those you could earn in a foreign stock market (use a foreign stock market index such as the Tokyo Nikkei 225 or the London FT 100). How do the foreign returns differ when measured in dollars from the local currency?

First, use the Web resources to get daily closing values of your selected stock indexes over a two-month period. In addition, obtain the daily exchange rate (against the dollar) for the country whose foreign stock market index you are monitoring, in terms of the U.S. dollar. Express the values of the foreign stock market index in U.S. dollar values by dividing the foreign stock market index by the current exchange rate, measured in units of foreign currency per dollar.

At the end of the two-month period, chart the index values of (1) the U.S. stock market, (2) the foreign stock market (measured in local foreign currency), and (3) the foreign stock market (measured in U.S. dollars).

Your Turn

Compare the returns in the foreign stock market to those in the U.S. stock market.
Why are the foreign stock market returns, measured in local currency terms, different from those measured in U.S. dollar terms?
What role do fluctuations in the exchange rate play?
Based on this exercise, if you were an investor trying to decide whether to invest in U.S. or foreign stock markets, what factors would you need to consider when making your decision?

Balancing the Federal Budget

Can you balance the budget? What programs would you cut? You can try balancing the U.S. federal budget using the *National Budget Simulator* (http://garnet.berkeley.edu:3333/budget/budget.html). The simulator actually uses 1995 federal budget figures, but it will give you a good feel for the tradeoffs in moving toward and maintaining a balanced budget.

Before you get started with a budget-cutting frenzy, familiarize yourself with the federal budget and the budget-making process using *A Citizen's Guide to the Federal Budget* (http://cher.eda.doc.gov/BudgetFY97/guidetoc.html). This guide contains information on sources of government revenue, government spending by category, recent data on budget deficits, and the budget-making process. After reading through the *Guide*, access the *National Budget Simulator* Web site and take a try at balancing the U.S. federal budget.

Your Turn

Given the conditions in 1995, what would it have taken to balance the budget? What areas of federal spending would you cut? Would you raise taxes? On whom? Be able to make a persuasive argument for your case.

It looks as though the budget will be balanced in fiscal year 1998, four years earlier than previously predicted.
Why were the predictions so far off?
Does the fact that the federal budget is currently balanced mean that budget deficit concerns are behind us? Why or why not?
Why is the National Budget Simulator exercise useful, even if the federal budget is currently balanced?

Determining the Natural Rate of Unemployment

This activity focuses on determining the lowest rate of unemployment that will lead to non-accelerating inflation, or finding an estimate of the natural rate of unemployment. The natural rate of unemployment may guide policymakers by providing them with a measure to determine whether the unemployment rate has fallen "too low," to a point where inflation rates may begin to rise. If so, policymakers can take actions to slow the economy down to reduce the risk of increasing inflation. There is much controversy, however, about the correct value of the natural rate of unemployment.

Find data on U.S. inflation rates and unemployment rates over the period 1962-1995 (see, for example, the statistical tables in the *Economic Report of the President*: **http://www.access.gpo.gov/su_docs/budget/index.html**).

- Make a table listing the year, the inflation rate for that year, and the unemployment rate for that year. Compute the year-to-year *changes* in the inflation rate, and list this information in an additional column.
- On a diagram with "change in the inflation rate from last year to the current year" on the vertical axis and "unemployment rate in the *previous* year" on the horizontal axis, plot the inflation change/unemployment combination for each year.
- Draw a straight line on the diagram that best "fits" the points on the diagram. Before doing this, consider which direction economic theory predicts the line should slope. Once the line is drawn, determine where the line crosses the horizontal axis.

Your Turn

Based on your analysis, answer the following questions:

What does this crossing point tell you, and what is its economic relevance?
How can this point help policymakers like the Federal Reserve in the current economic situation?
Are there any problems using this "point estimate" of the natural rate for policy guidance?
What is the range of unemployment rates consistent with "low" inflation rate changes – say, less than 1% from year to year?
Explain why this causes difficulties for policymakers like the Federal Reserve, who must make decisions about whether to leave the economy alone or raise interest rates to slow down spending and production.
What might cause the "horizontal intercept" (where your line crosses the horizontal axis) in these diagrams to shift to the left or right? Relate this to current economic conditions in the economy.

Note: This exercise is based on the article, "The NAIRU, Unemployment, and Monetary Policy" by Douglas Staiger, James H. Stock, and Mark W. Watson, *Journal of Economic Perspectives*, (Volume 11, Number 1) Winter 1997, pp. 33-49.

Chapter 6
Online Information About Careers, Graduate School, and Jobs

On the Internet, finding information about careers is just a mouse-click away. Whether you're looking for a job that can put your economics skills to use, thinking about graduate school or law school, or simply exploring career options, you can gather a great deal of information without leaving your keyboard. You can learn about potential employers, exchange ideas with other job seekers, and enlarge your circle of contacts, all by launching your Web browser.

How to Research Careers on the Internet

A good way to start your online hunt is by researching various occupations and industries that sound appealing and that match your interests and background. For example, you might want to obtain general information about future job prospects for economists or investigate related occupations that rely on the analytical skills you are developing in your economics courses.

A great place to start is the *Occupational Outlook Handbook*, from the U.S. Department of Labor. This multi-faceted site describes a wide range of occupations, detailing each job's duties, training requirements, employment trends, and future prospects. For the latest news about employment projections, earnings, and the effect of regional economic conditions on job opportunities, you can also check the news releases posted online by the U.S. Bureau of Labor Statistics. The Web sites for these two resources follow:

Occupational Outlook Handbook
http://stats.bls.gov/ocohome.htm

U.S. Bureau of Labor Statistics News Releases
http://stats.bls.gov/newsrels.htm

In addition, many state employment offices maintain Web sites bursting with information about occupations, industries, wages, and many other topics. You can locate your state's job service site by launching your favorite Internet search engine and using "state employment service" or a similar phrase as your keyword. Once you find your state's site, be sure to explore each hyperlink—you never know where these connections will lead you.

For example, the Career Resource Library on the New York State Department of Labor Web site (http://ny.jobsearch.org/library.htm) contains a wealth of hyperlinks to sites about state and regional employment trends; national, statewide, and local wage rates; industry descriptions; résumé preparation; training and education; job applications; and interviewing (see Figure 6.1). Even job-seekers outside New York will be interested in the general guidance available on this site.

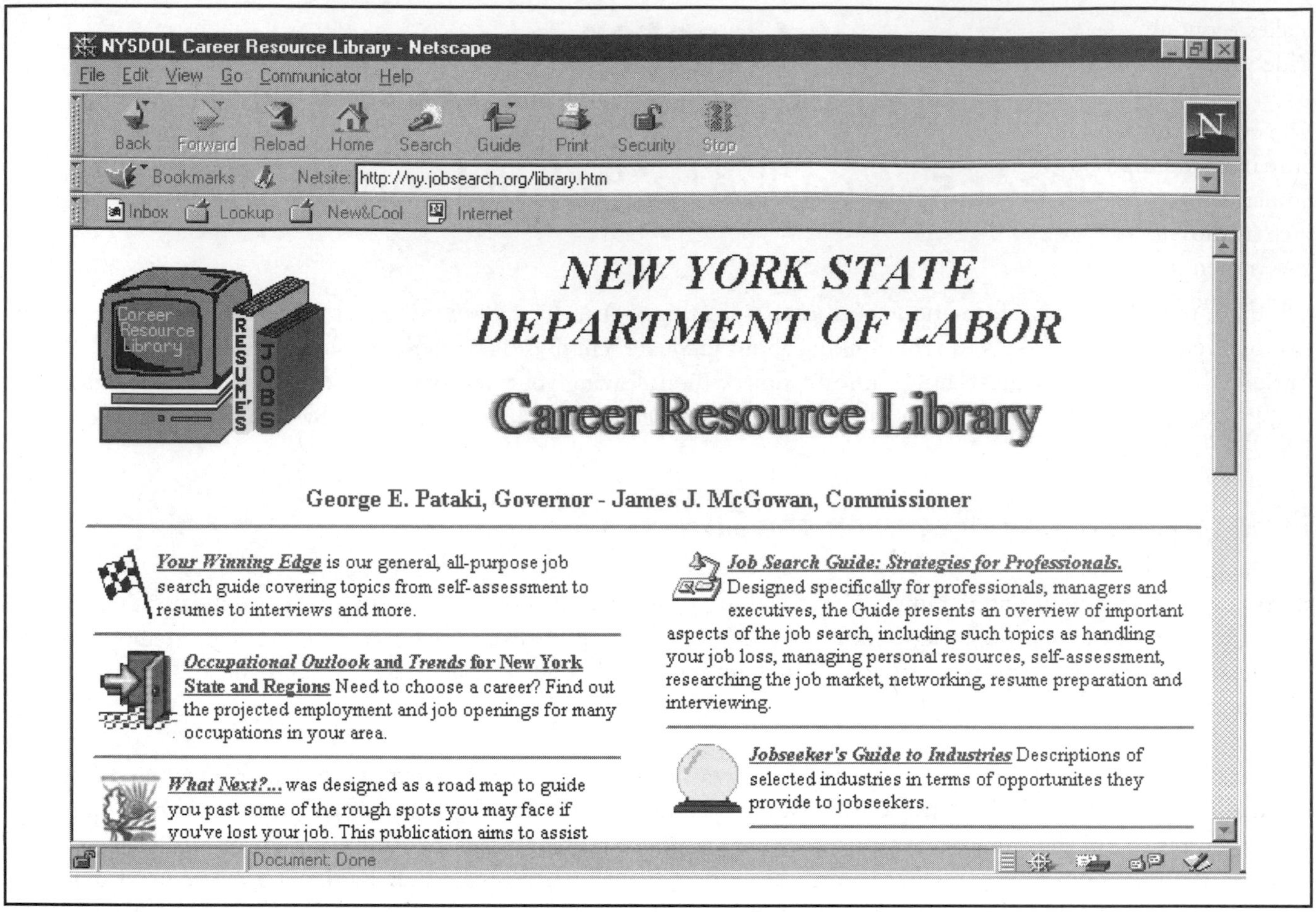

Figure 6.1. Check out the career research library at the Web site of the New York State Department of Labor.

Finally, be sure to take advantage of your school's career services, which are often available online through the campus placement office. You may want to browse other university career-counseling Web sites for more information about various occupations. Here are just two samples:

Career Exploration Links (University of California at Berkeley)
http://www.uhs.berkeley.edu/CareerLibrary/links/occup.cfm

Exploring Occupations" (University of Manitoba)
http://www.umanitoba.ca/counselling/careers.html

Both of these sites offer hyperlinks to pages describing dozens of occupations.

What can I do with a career in economics?

College students often overlook economics as a major. Why? Many students have had little exposure to formal economic training prior to college. In addition, students often have preconceived notions that economics is "hard" or requires too much analytical reasoning. But it is precisely the development of this analytical reasoning ability that makes economics such an attractive major for students considering law school, graduate school, or employment in a wide variety of fields.

The critical thinking skills gained from economic analysis provide an excellent foundation for graduate study not only in economics, but also in public policy, international studies, finance, management, and many other disciplines. Students who major in economics are among the most competitive for jobs that require superior analytical ability, such as those in investment banking, transportation, insurance, management consulting, and local, state, and federal government agencies. Students who complement their formal training in economics with skills in statistics, mathematics, and computer science are particularly attractive to potential employers.

What do economists do? About a third of all economists work in private industry, running background research on particular industries or firms, forecasting future economic conditions, analyzing the effects of changes in federal or state regulations on a firm's costs and revenues, and exploring the economic effects of strategic management decisions. A large number of economists are also hired by local, state, or federal government agencies; the federal government is the single largest employer of economists in the United States. Economists working in government may prepare economic impact statements, generate economic forecasts, analyze the effects of proposed regulation changes, assess international economic conditions, and predict the effects of monetary or fiscal policy, among a variety of other functions. The *Occupational Outlook Handbook*, which we mentioned earlier, includes detailed information about careers in economics.

According to the 1998-99 *Handbook*, jobs for economists are expected to grow "as fast as the average for all occupations through the year 2006." In terms of salaries, the *Handbook* reports that in 1997 "persons with a bachelor's degree in economics received offers averaging $31,300 a year; for those with a bachelor's degrees in marketing, $27,900."

Graduate School and Law School Information

Not everyone looks for a job immediately after college. For many of you, undergraduate education is the first step toward the goal of a law degree, an MBA degree, or a graduate degree in economics. The Internet provides a number of Web sites to help determine which graduate schools and programs best match your interests. It also helps you prepare for graduate school and law school admission tests.

If you're thinking about graduate school or law school, realize that law schools, business schools, and graduate schools in economics require entrance examinations that vary by discipline. Begin exploring graduate program options early to become familiar with the required exams and the types of graduate programs that are available. The sites listed below provide valuable information on exam dates and registration deadlines, practice exams, online registration for tests, links to information about universities, programs, financial aid, and much more!

Graduate Record Exam (GRE)
http://www.gre.com

Graduate Management Admissions Test (GMAT)
http://www.gmat.org

Law School Admissions Test (LSAT)
http://www.lsat.org

Princeton Review
http://www.review.com

U.S. News Colleges and Careers Center
http://www.usnews.com/usnews/edu/home.htm

Finding Job Openings on the Internet

The Internet has become a powerful job-seeking tool as more and more employers begin to post their job openings on the Web. How can you best put the power of the Web to use in getting a job?

Online Services

Some of the major online services and search tools are good places to start when looking for job openings on the Internet. In addition to finding career-planning advice, job postings, résumé preparation tips, and other useful information, you may also be able to join a job-search newsgroup, participate in an online chat about how to interview well, or read messages posted by other people in the job market.

For instance, visit Yahoo! and go to its employment area, which is located under the business category (http://www.yahoo.com/Business/Employment/). On this page, you can scroll through a variety of help-wanted classified ads, post your résumé for employers to consider, or drop into an interesting job-related online chat. Events and job openings change daily, so check back often.

Virtual Career Fairs

Another way to find job openings on the Web is to visit virtual career fairs, where employers and job-seekers meet online. As in any career fair, you can find out more about participating employers, explore their immediate and anticipated job openings, submit your résumé for consideration, and (sometimes) have an initial Cyberspace interview. Look for career fairs listed at sites such as:

The Monster Board
http://www.monster.com

Yahoo
http://www.yahoo.com/Business_and_Economy/Employment/Jobs/Job_Fairs/

Virtual Job Fair
http://www.vjf.com

Job Databanks

Help-wanted classified ads and job databanks are available on a variety of Web sites. Best Jobs USA (http://www.bestjobsusa.com), a Web site maintained by *Employment Review* magazine, invites job-seekers to search its listings of jobs by state, by category, by company name, or by special skill. You may also want to bookmark the career Web site maintained by the *Wall Street Journal* (http://careers.wsj.com/). Here, you can use the *Job Seek* function to search posted job openings by industry, by type of job, by company, and by location. If you choose, you can add your name to an e-mail list at this site so you will be alerted when new employers and new features become available. A sampling of other useful job databanks include:

CareerMosaic
http://www.service.com/cm/cm1.html

College Grad Job Hunter
http://www.collegegrad.com/

E-Span
http://www.espan.com/

FedWorld Federal Jobs Search (Federal Jobs)
http://www.fedworld.gov/jobs/jobsearch.html

USA Jobs (Federal Jobs)
http://www.usajobs.opm.gov/

The Online Career Center
http://www.occ.com/occ/

America's Job Bank
http://www.ajb.dni.us/

Newspaper Advertisements

Newspaper classified ads, a traditional source of leads for new jobs, are increasingly common on the Web. For example, if you live in the Boston area—or if you want to relocate there—you may want to search the *Boston Globe's* online employment classifieds (**http://careers.boston.com/**). Newspapers in other major metropolitan areas provide similar services. You can use *Yahoo!* or another search tool to locate the Web sites of newspapers in specific cities. In addition, hyperlinks to leading newspapers are available at the Info Service Web site (**http://info-s.com/paper6.html**) and at Ecola, which serves as a gateway to dozens of U.S. publications (**http://www.ecola.com/news/press/na/us/**).

Some sites compile listings of help wanted ads drawn from numerous newspapers. One good example is the CareerPath Web site (**http://www.careerpath.com**). This site also lists job openings that have been posted on company Web sites, a time-saving feature that allows you to search job listings by state, name of employer, industry, and/or type of job. Another example is the National Ad Search site (**http://www.nationaladsearch.com/about.htm**), which offers thousands of help-wanted display ads from newspapers in more than 50 metropolitan areas.

Company Web Sites

Once you have narrowed your search to a particular occupation or industry, you can begin to study potential employers. If you know the names of companies in your targeted field, you can use an Internet search tool to locate their Web sites. As you investigate any potential employer's Web site, look carefully for a hyperlink to that company's listing of job vacancies. These hyperlinks may be labeled "career opportunities," "recruitment," or some similar title.

Another way to locate company Web sites is through hyperlinks on the larger career Web sites such as Espan (**http://www.espan**) and Career Mosaic (**http://www.careermosaic.com**). For example, you can get information about companies that recruit from the Espan site by clicking on each employer's hyperlink. In some cases, the hyperlink leads to the company's regular Web site. In other cases, the hyperlink leads to a special recruitment page. For example, if you click on the name of Allstate on Espan's employer page, you will be connected to the insurance company's career site, which covers career opportunities, internships, benefits, and general information.

Résumé Databanks

If you want to post your résumé and invite prospective employers to find you, take time to investigate the growing number of résumé databanks available on the Internet. You can find listings of the largest databanks—as well as those that specialize in particular occupations—by checking career Web sites such as Job Hunt (**http://www.job-hunt.org/resume.shtml**) and Job Resources (**http://solimar1.stanford.edu/**), which was started by students from Stanford University.

Employers that recruit online generally prefer to receive electronic résumés rather than the printed résumés. The next section shows how to prepare your résumé for electronic submission to employers and databanks.

How to Present Yourself on the Internet

Just as you are using your PC to search for employers and jobs via the Internet, a growing number of employers are using computers to store and search through all the résumés they receive from applicants. Instead of spending hours sifting through a mountain of cover letters and printed résumés, a manager can now enter a few key words or phrases to describe the required skills and qualifications for a particular job opening. In short order, the computer will bring up a listing of all the electronic résumés in the database that fit those exact specifications. Only applicants whose résumés are in the computer system will be considered for such job opportunities—which is why *you* need an electronic résumé.

Keep it Simple

How can you best present yourself in Cyberspace? If you have already created a résumé using a word-processing program, a few simple changes will get it into shape for submission to company computer systems and commercial résumé databanks. Start by opening the file containing your résumé, then saving it as a plain ASCII text file. Change the name, if you want, to distinguish this text-only version from the fully formatted version.

Because text-only files cannot accommodate fancy fonts, be sure your résumé appears in one simple font and one font size. Remove any formatting such as boldface, underlining, and italics. Also remove justification, tables, rules, and columns. If you have tabs in your document, remove them and use the space bar to align your text. Then change every bullet to an asterisk or a lower-case letter *o*, as shown in Figure 6.2. Even if you are e-mailing your résumé directly to an individual at a firm, it is best to keep the formatting as simple as possible. You don't know what e-mail and word-processing package will be used on the other end, and the résumé that you worked so hard to create may end up as a garbled mess.

Roberto Cortez

5687 Crosswoods Drive
Falls Church, Virginia 22046
Home: (703) 987-0086 Office: (703) 549-6624

OBJECTIVE

Accounting management position requiring a knowledge of international finance

EXPERIENCE

March 1993 to present	Staff Accountant/Financial Analyst, Inter-American Imports(Alexandria, VA) • Prepare accounting reports for wholesale giftware importer with annual sales of $15 million • Audit financial transactions with suppliers in 12 Latin American countries • Created a computerized model to adjust accounts for fluctuations in currency exchange rates • Negotiated joint-venture agreements with major suppliers in Mexico and Columbia
October 1989 to March 1993	Staff Accountant, Monsanto Agricultural Chemicals (Mexico City, Mexico) • Handled budgeting, billing, and credit-processing functions for the Mexico City branch • Audited travel/entertainment expenses for Monsanto's 30-member Latin American sales force • Assisted in launching an online computer system (IBM)

EDUCATION

1989 to 1993	MBA with emphasis on international business George Mason University (Fairfax, Virginia)
1985 to 1989	BBA, Accounting Universidad Naçional Autónoma de Mexico (Mexico City, Mexico)

INTERCULTURAL QUALIFICATIONS

- Born and raised in Mexico City; became U.S. citizen in 1991
- Fluent in Spanish and German
- Traveled extensively in Latin America

References available on request

Résumé Submitted in Confidence

Figure 6.2. This résumé is a good model for how to prepare your own electronic résumé as you use the Web to learn more about job opportunities.

What to Include

The first line of your résumé should contain only your full name. Type your street address, phone and fax numbers, and e-mail address on separate lines below your name. Next, count the number of characters in each line—and create a new line whenever the number of characters (including spaces) exceeds 65. This ensures that your electronic résumé will look neat when a potential employer brings it up on the screen.

Knowing that employers search their résumé databases according to key words, you should include a *key word* section near the top of your résumé. To do this, compile a list of nouns that describe your job-related skills and abilities. Some of these nouns may already be contained in your résumé, but you will also want to highlight them by positioning them in the key word section.

For example, depending on your work experience, you will want to include appropriate job titles (such as "supervisor" or "team leader") in the key word section. Similarly, if you have experience with a specialized area such as exchange rates, list the phrase "exchange rates" in your key word section. Be sure to highlight your full range of accomplishments, including such skills as fluency in other languages and any official certification courses you have completed.

Once you have completed work on your résumé, be sure to save it again as an ASCII plain text file. If you prepare separate electronic résumés for different employers or job openings, save those in separate ASCII files so you can easily access them when needed. To be sure that your electronic résumé looks good, copy and paste it into an e-mail message to yourself or to a friend. Once the e-mail message is received, you will be able to spot and correct any formatting errors.

Remember that all the usual rules about writing a good résumé also apply to your electronic résumé: showcase your strongest qualifications; summarize your work experience with an emphasis on results and achievements; mention relevant activities and talents; and use correct spelling and grammar. Above all, be honest. If you misrepresent your background, you may find yourself out of a job when your new employer finds out.

Examples and Sources of Information on Electronic Résumés

To get an idea of what other traditional and electronic résumés look like, you may want to browse the career sites, which often feature sample résumés. In addition, you can launch your news reader and access the newsgroup misc.jobs.resumes, where you will find many résumés posted.

Also, seek out Web sites that offer general advice about résumés, both traditional and electronic. Among the many academic sites you can browse are the site sponsored by Purdue University (http://owl.english.purdue.edu/Files/35.html) and the site sponsored by the College of William & Mary (http://www.wm.edu/csrv/career/stualum/resmdir/contents.html).

A wealth of information about electronic résumés is also available at the following Web sites (see Figure 6.3), which feature job openings and hyperlinks to a variety of career development resources.

America's Job Bank
http://www.ajb.dni.us/html/eresume.html#prep

Online Career Center
http://www.occ.com/occ/jlk/howtoeresume.html

Resumix
http://www.resumix.com/resume/resumeindex.html

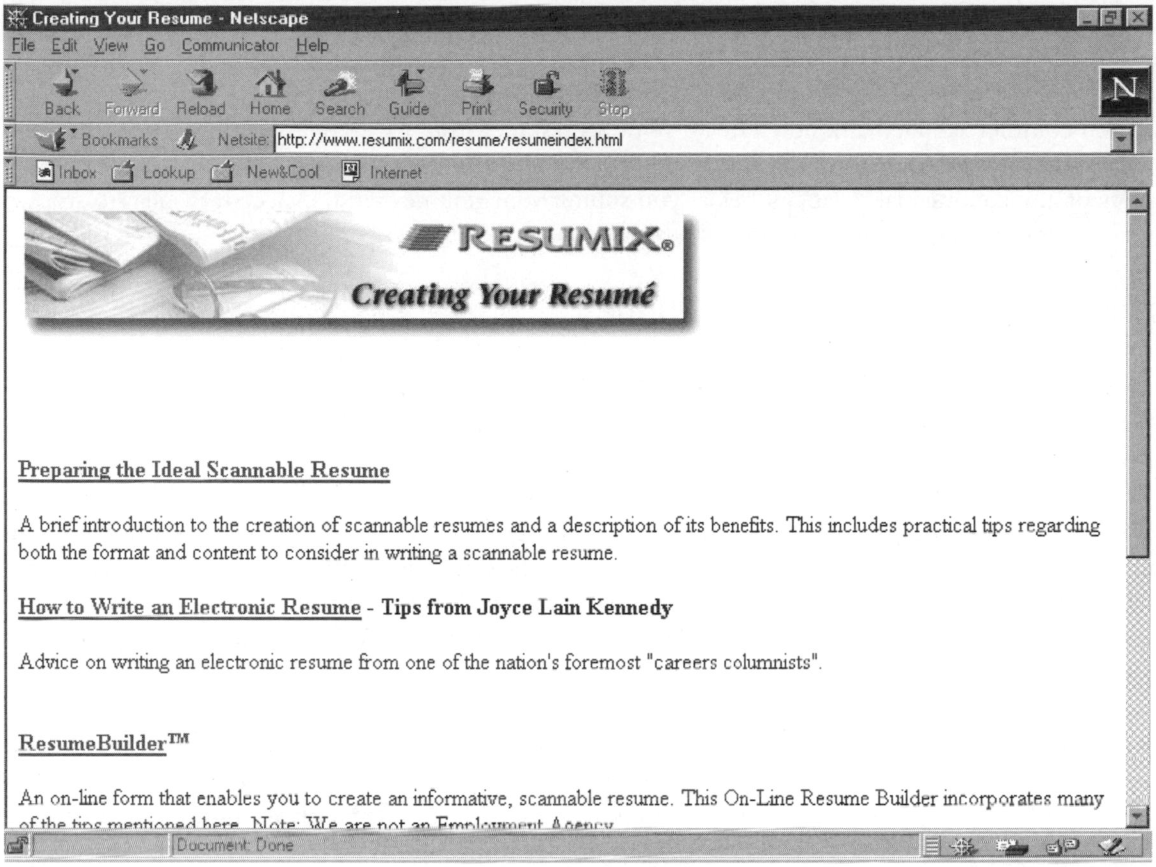

Figure 6.3. Resumix®, which provides human resource software solutions for large corporations, also offers instructions and helpful tips on how to prepare the most effective electronic résumés.

Posting Your Résumé to a Résumé Databank

Once you have polished your electronic résumé, should you submit it to one or more résumé databanks? Uploading your résumé to be included in a larger databank of résumés is not the same as sending your résumé to a single employer's résumé database. The employer is going to keep your résumé in its proprietary computer system, to be accessed only by company personnel who are searching for applicants to fill job openings. Commercial résumé databanks, however, are open to many employers, which raises several issues for you to consider.

Be aware that submitting your résumé to a commercial databank makes your private information available to many people. If you have security concerns about publicizing your home address and phone number, you may want to omit these details—or follow the advice of one expert, who recommends arranging for a post office box and answering service with a separate phone number to handle inquiries during the job-search period.

In addition, before you post your electronic résumé on any databank, find out who is allowed to access the résumés. Also ask whether you will be notified when an employer requests your résumé—and whether you can limit access to prevent specific organizations (such as your current employer) from requesting your résumé.

Another issue to consider is how often you are allowed to update your résumé, and whether you will be charged for doing so. At some point, you may need to correct a spelling error or add a new skill you recently acquired. If you are expected to pay for updates, continue looking until you find a suitable databank that permits free updates.

Finally, ask each commercial databank how often it removes résumés from its system. Employers want to see only up-to-date résumés, which is why some databanks get rid of older résumés after a certain number of months. So investigate the policy of any commercial databank before you submit your résumé—and, if necessary, plan to submit updated résumés at regular intervals throughout your job search.

Contacting Employers Directly (Online)

Now that your electronic résumé is ready, you can move full speed ahead with your job search, checking both traditional and Internet sources for employment openings. When you find an intriguing job opening, carefully follow the employer's instructions for applying electronically.

Some employers that post job openings on the Internet require applicants to fill out an online form, typing in name, address, and other details. In many cases, you will notice a large box near the bottom of the online form. This is where you are expected to paste the plain text version of your résumé (after copying it from the ASCII file). The employer may also ask you to insert a reference code or word somewhere on the form to identify the opening for which you are applying.

At times, you will find that a job opening posted on the employer's Web site is accompanied by a hyperlink that leads to a pre-addressed e-mail message form. Again, follow the employer's instructions for completing the message. If you are instructed to type in a job title or reference number, enter this information according to the employer's instructions, then follow the employer's exact directions for submitting your résumé.

If you are responding to a help-wanted ad in a newspaper or some other medium, you can apply by e-mail if the employer includes an e-mail address. Launch your Web browser or Internet communication program, bring up a blank message screen, and type the employer's e-mail address in the *To* field. If the ad includes a job title or reference number, always include that information in the *Subject* field.

Next, type a very brief cover letter in the *Message* field, explaining that you are applying for the advertised position and stating your strongest qualifications (see Figure 6.4). You can't actually sign your letter, but you can type a polite complimentary closing, press the *Enter* key twice, and type your full name. Finally, copy and paste your electronic résumé below the cover letter in the *Message* field. Take a minute to reread the message—checking spelling and spacing—before you actually press the *Send* button.

Cover Letters and Follow-up

For more information about writing an effective cover letter, point your browser to Brandeis University's Hiatt Career Development Center Web site (**http://www.brandeis.edu/hiatt/web_data/hiatt_cover_letter.html**) or the State University of New York at Buffalo's Career Planning & Placement Web site (**http://www.ub-careers.buffalo.edu/career/resume/coverlet.html**).

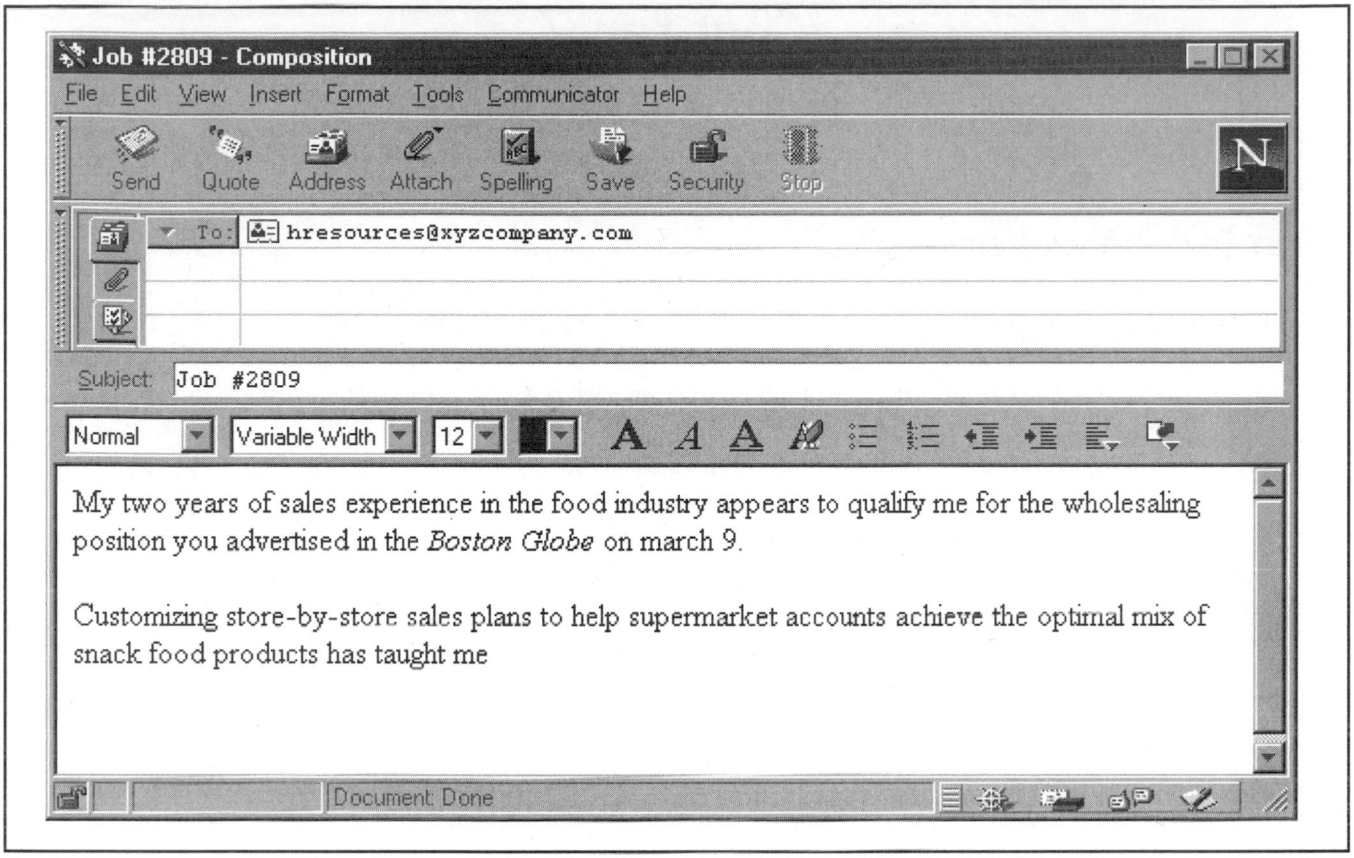

Figure 6.4. Your can use the e-mail feature on your browser to communicate with potential employers.

Never send your electronic résumé as an attachment to an e-mail message unless an employer specifically requests this transmission method. Given the diversity of word-processing programs in the business world, your résumé may not be compatible with the employer's software—which means that your résumé will not become part of that company's database.

Companies that encourage e-mail submission of résumés are generally receptive to e-mail messages as follow-ups to job-search activities such as interviews. Rather than print and mail a thank-you letter after an interview, for example, you can send your company contact an e-mail message with the same information. When composing a thank-you message, refer to the interview in your *Subject* line by typing "Thank you for the October 26 interview " or a similar brief phrase in the subject line.

After you have typed the body of your message, include a business-like complimentary closing, press the *Enter* key twice, and type your full name. Then type your address, your phone and fax numbers, and your e-mail address on separate lines directly below your name. After all, you want to make it as easy and convenient as possible for potential employers to contact you.

Good luck!

Chapter 7
Distance Learning

What is Distance Learning?

Imagine an educational system in which you can take a course, submit an assignment, even interact with your instructor and classmates without stepping into a real classroom—that's distance learning. As the name implies, students are physically separated from instructors (and often from each other) in a distance learning arrangement. The purpose is to bring the learning to the student, rather than bringing the student to the learning—providing more flexibility and more options for personal and professional growth.

As a student, you can participate in distance learning in a variety of ways. In some programs, you receive instruction and assignments via the Internet, using e-mail, audio streaming, video clips, group chats, or other techniques; in other programs, you watch your instructor on videotape, video conference, or television. Your alternatives for distance learning will depend on the provider of the course you select.

In early distance learning programs, students watched televised lectures (on regularly-scheduled programs with titles such as *Sunrise Semester*) and then mailed completed assignments to the college for grading and credit. Today, some form of distance learning is available at more than half of all four-year colleges and universities in the United States—and many offer degree programs entirely by Internet.

For example, the Colorado Electronic Community College (**http://www.ccconline.org**) offers an Internet-only associate degree program. Similarly, the University of Phoenix (**http://www.uophx.edu.online**) offers Internet-only undergraduate and graduate degrees. These types of programs allow students to use the Internet for almost everything, from ordering textbooks and filling out financial aid forms to downloading course materials and taking quizzes.

Distance learning is also becoming more popular at colleges and universities around the world, from Aston University in the United Kingdom (**http://www.les.aston.ac.uk/home.html**) to Macquarie University in Australia (**http://www.elm.mq.edu.au**).

Colleges are not the only sources of distance learning programs. Employers have begun to embrace distance learning in its many forms. As one example, the Tennessee Valley Authority offers career enrichment courses by videotape and by self-paced computer training, in addition to its traditional classroom courses. As another example, employees of GTE Corporation can attend educational videoconferences on personal finance as well as participate in job-related courses.

Professional organizations such as the Illinois Association of Realtors are also using distance learning on the Internet to provide continuing education training to their members. And distance learning is now being developed by some companies as a profit-making venture. ZDNet University (**http://www.zdu.com**) is a good example. An offshoot of Ziff-Davis, which publishes magazines on information technology, ZDNet University offers courses on Internet technology and its business applications.

Distance is no object when you are able to access learning materials via the Internet. Whether a course originates in another city, state, or country, all students receive the same lectures, assignments, and attention. As a result, a student in the United States can sign up for an education class at the University of Birmingham in England (**http://sun4.bham.ac.uk**), while a student in California can log onto a course in speechwriting offered by Syracuse University Continuing Education OnLine in New York state (**http://www.suce.syr.edu/online/**).

Wherever you are, whatever you want to learn, you can probably find a distance learning course somewhere in the world to meet your needs.

Advantages and Disadvantages

Distance learning on the Internet has many advantages. At the top of the list is the broad array of choices. You can earn a degree, obtain continuing education credits, sharpen your work skills, prepare for a new job or career, stay abreast of fast-changing technology, even master a new subject for personal enrichment—all without leaving your keyboard.

Easy access is another major advantage. As long as you have the right computer hardware and software as well as a connection to the Internet, you can be a distance learning student. Just log onto the course's Web site to download the latest lecture, or enter the designated chat room for a Cyberspace exchange of ideas. If you have a laptop computer with modem, you can easily send in your course assignments from home, office, or almost anywhere.

Most of the time, distance learning on the Internet allows you to work at your own pace, an important advantage for people who are juggling school and work responsibilities and those whose schedules can change from day to day. Rather than having to be in the classroom at a particular time, distance learning students can usually access a Web site at any hour to read new assignments or e-mail the instructor with questions.

Distance learning on the Internet can save you money, even though some undergraduate and graduate courses are more costly than traditional classroom courses. For example, tuition for one credit hour at the Colorado Electronic Community College is more than twice the price of one credit hour of on-campus study. Still, by using the Internet for distance learning, you completely avoid charges for room and board (or the cost of traveling to class), which can represent a significant savings.

Of course, distance learning on the Internet has disadvantages, as well. One key disadvantage is the lack of live interaction with the instructor and with classmates. If you thrive on classroom debate or prefer to have your questions answered immediately, you may not like having to type your comments or wait for an e-mailed response.

Some programs have addressed this issue by arranging for periodic desktop videoconferencing. Students and instructors place small video cameras on their computer monitors and speak into microphones to participate in group discussions during a desktop videoconference session. Students can see the instructor, the instructor can see the students, and everybody can hear every comment.

Another disadvantage is the need for access to an appropriately configured personal computer and an Internet connection in order to take an online course. In response, some schools are inviting their distance learning students to use the computer facilities on campus or at regional satellite centers.

Overall, distance learning is best suited to students who are motivated to assume responsibility for their own learning. You must be willing to log onto the course Web site at regular intervals; download and review instructional materials; and post your questions or ask for additional help.

Remember, some courses require students to visit chat rooms for group discussions; some mandate frequent or lengthy homework projects; others expect students to read and comment on classmates' reports and projects. You have to be ready to invest sufficient time and effort to meet all these course requirements. You must also have the flexibility to deal with the occasional technical glitches that can crop up. Only you can decide whether distance learning is right for you.

How to Find Information About Distance Learning

In an earlier chapter, you learned how to search for information using directories and search engines. Now you can apply your search skills to scour the World Wide Web for information about distance learning classes and resources.

A Yahoo! Search

First, try using Yahoo! to conduct this search. Start by connecting to the Internet and launching your Web browser. In the location box (designated as "Go to" in Netscape Navigator), type in the address for Yahoo! (**http://www.yahoo.com**) and press the enter key on your keyboard.

Once the Yahoo! home page appears (see Figure 7.1), you will see a search box near the top of the screen. Type in the words "distance learning" in quotation marks and click on the search button to begin your search for Web documents containing that exact phrase.

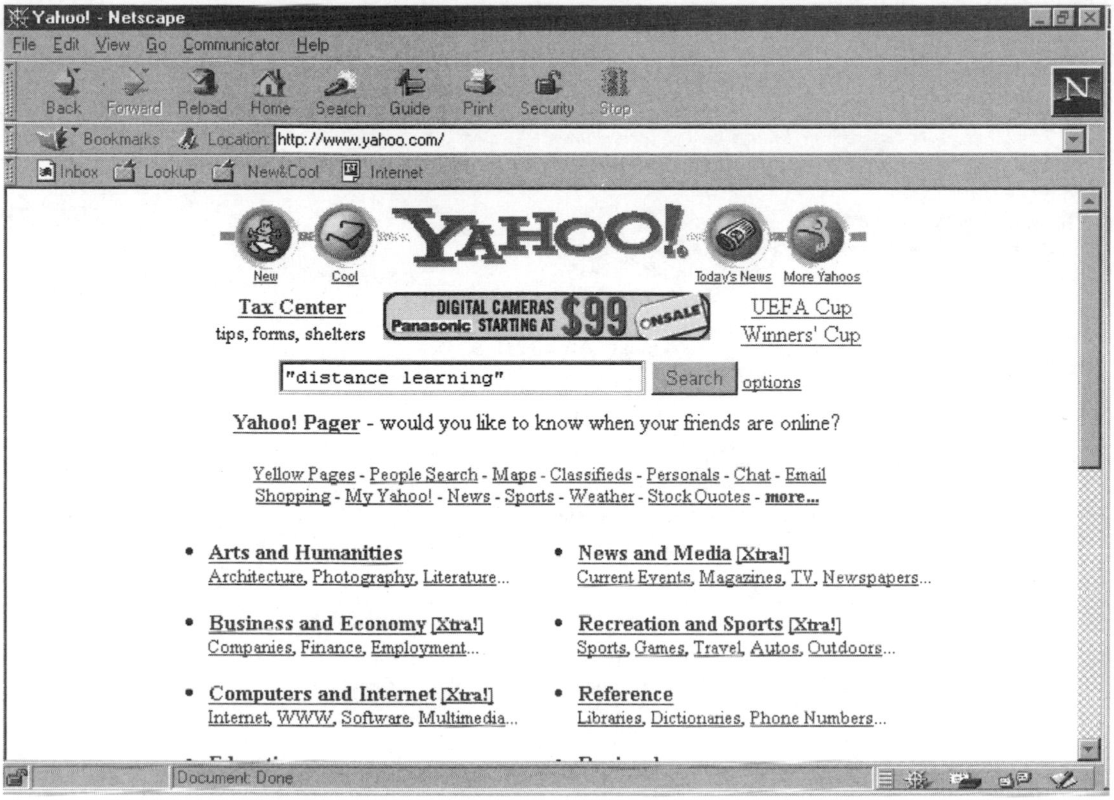

Figure 7.1. Type in the words "distance learning" in the search box on Yahoo!'s home page and begin a wide-ranging tour of the Internet.

Within a few seconds, you will be presented with a listing of category matches and Web sites, arranged alphabetically. Depending on your particular interest, you can click on the hyperlinks that lead to more information about specific types of courses or geographic locations of institutions and sponsors offering distance learning opportunities. Bear in mind that Web sites and hyperlinks are subject to change, so your search results are likely to differ from the examples and illustrations in this guide.

The broadest category on this initial list is titled "Education: Distance Learning" (see Figure 7.2). Click on that hyperlink to see a more detailed listing of distance learning resources.

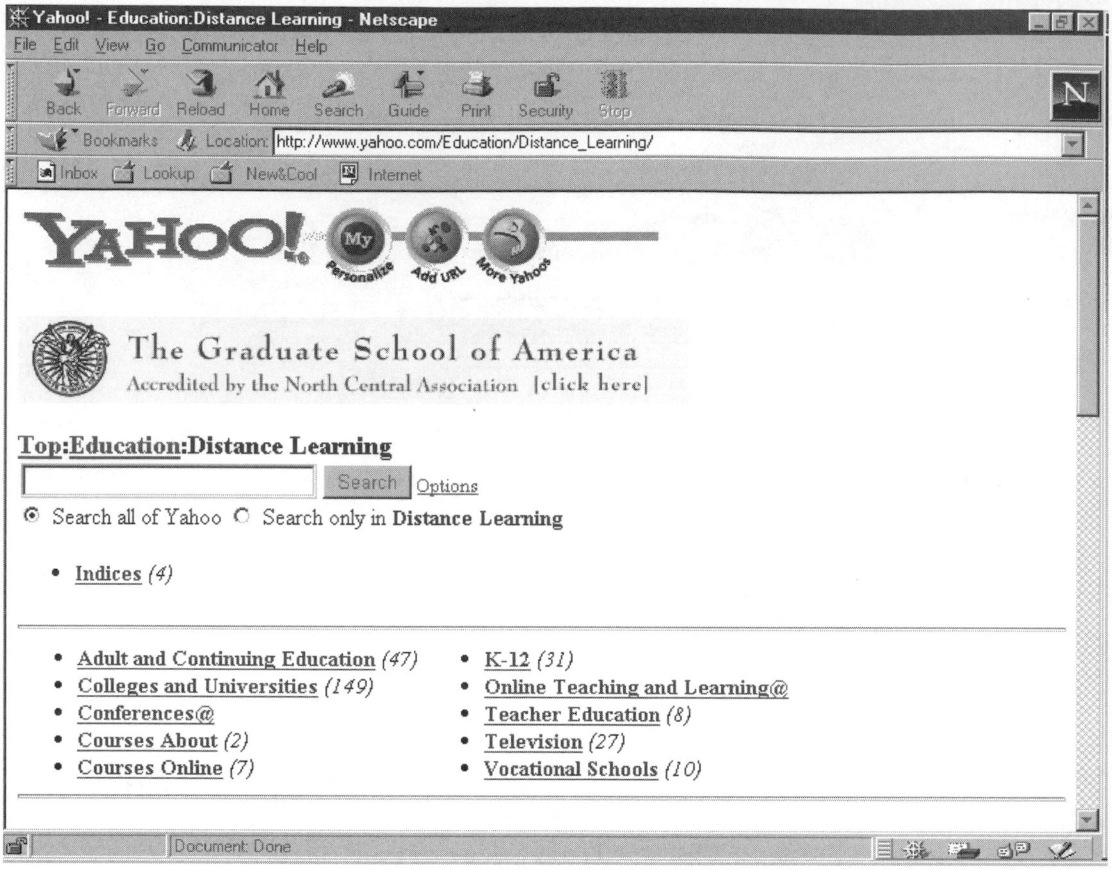

Figure 7.2. From this Yahoo! page you can click on the hyperlinks that will carry you to categories of courses, colleges, and other education opportunities.

This page in the Yahoo! directory serves as a general guide to all types of distance learning courses. Notice that you can click on hyperlinks for categories of courses, including adult and continuing education; colleges and universities; and other types of courses. The number in parentheses next to the category name indicates how many hyperlinks are available for that subject.

Below the categories are individual hyperlinks to additional resources, including sites that list distance learning opportunities and sites that offer information about distance learning theory and techniques. You can click on any hyperlink, explore the contents, and then click the *Back* button on the browser toolbar to jump back to the Yahoo! search results and explore more hyperlinks. Also, use the Yahoo! search facility to quickly find specific words or phrases (such as "business") embedded in the categories and hyperlinks on a particular page—or throughout the entire Yahoo! site.

What if you want to find out more about colleges and universities offering distance learning courses? Simply click on that hyperlink in the Yahoo! search results, and you will be presented with several subcategories, including community colleges and graduate programs, plus an alphabetical listing of sources for classes and more information. Now you can click on any hyperlink to go immediately to that site.

A Metacrawler Search

When you search for the same phrase in another search tool, your results will be somewhat different. To see how this works, try using Metacrawler to search for distance learning courses. Metacrawler conducts a simultaneous search on six directories and search engines: Webcrawler, Excite, Yahoo!, Infoseek, Lycos, and AltaVista.

You can reach the Metacrawler Web site through your Web browser by typing the address (**http://www.metacrawler.com**) in the location box. With Metacrawler's home page on your screen (see Figure 7.3), type in the phrase "distance learning" in the search box, click the "as a phrase" option, select "the Web," and click the "search" button.

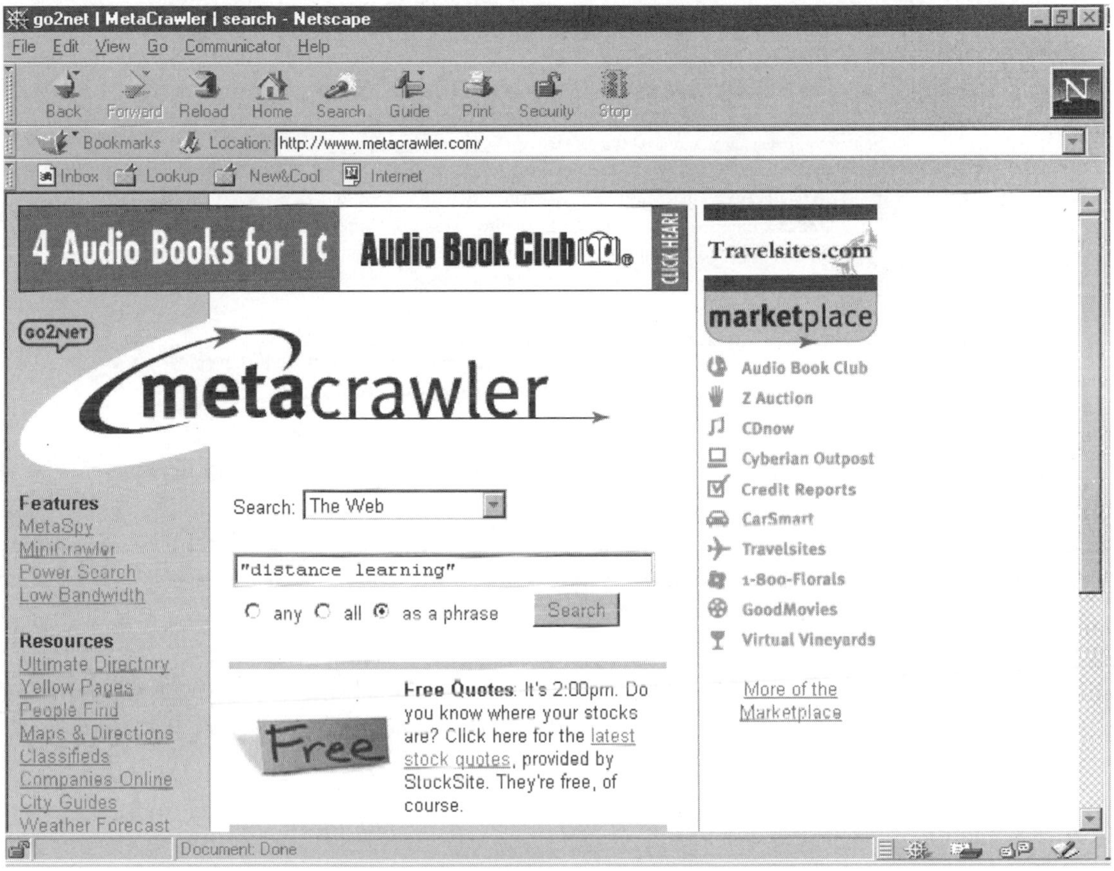

Figure 7.3. Metacrawler provides results drawn from a search through six different directories and search engines.

A few seconds will pass as Metacrawler compiles the answers it is receiving from each of the six search tools. Then you will see a detailed listing of the results, ranked according to the numeric score that indicates the relevancy of each site (see Figure 7.4). You can now read the description of each site before you click on the hyperlink. Metacrawler speeds you through the results by highlighting the search word or phrase in bold in the title or description of each site.

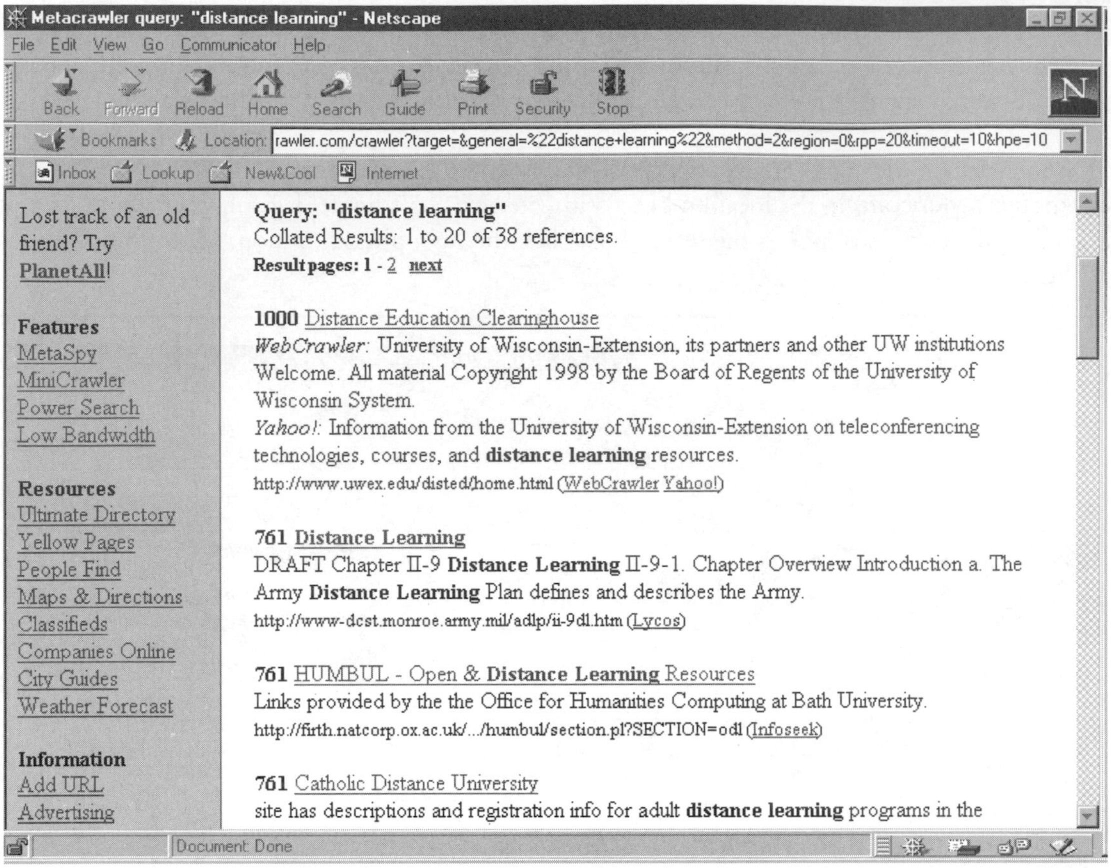

Figure 7.4. This screen shows you the first twenty of thirty-eight references Metacrawler found while searching "distance learning."

A Newsgroup Search

You can also use Webcrawler to locate newsgroups about distance learning. Simply type "distance learning" in the search box, select "newsgroups," and then click the "search button." The results will show descriptions of messages that have been posted to newsgroups (see Figure 7.5).

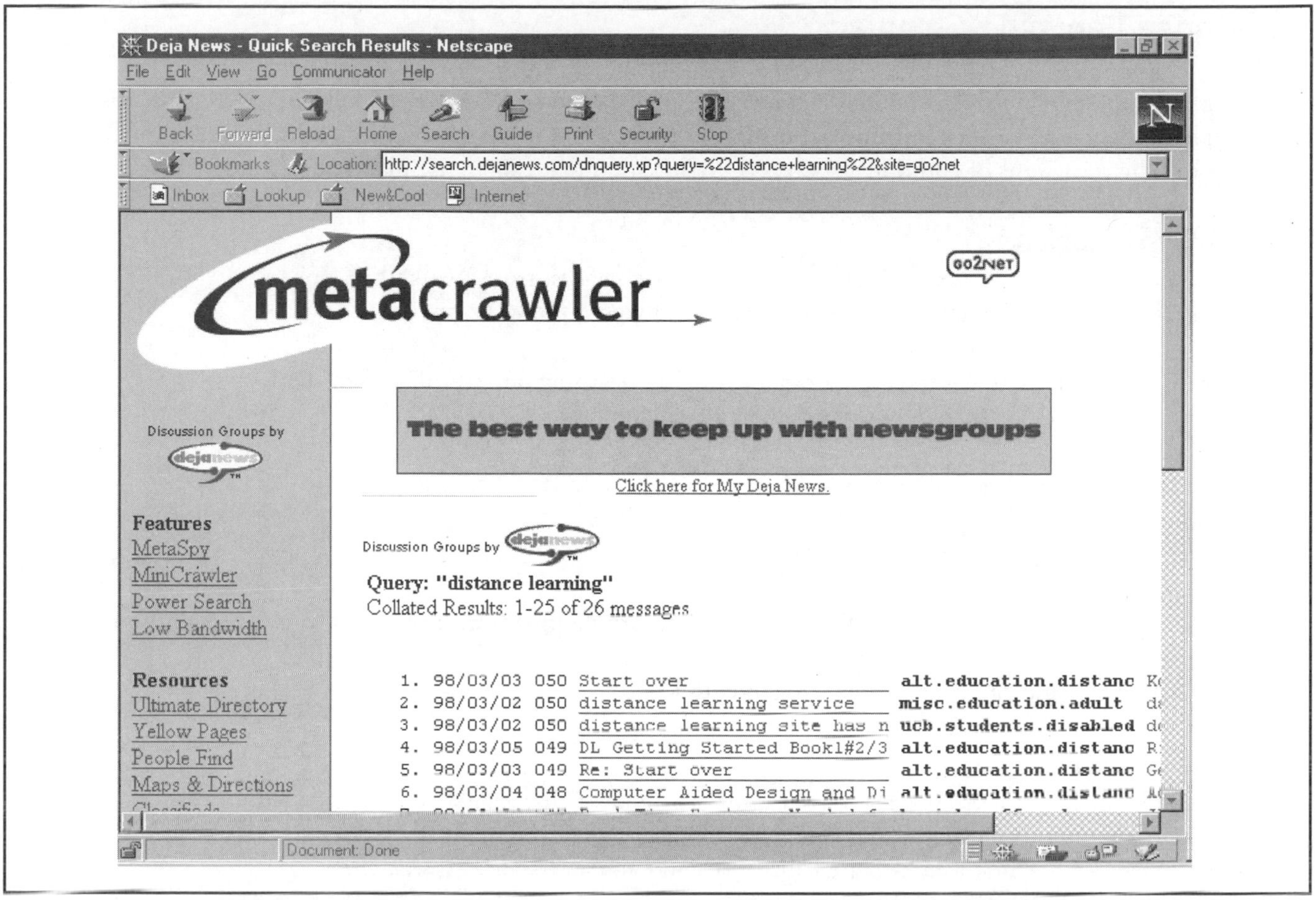

Figure 7.5. Metacrawler also searches for newsgroups. This screen shows some newsgroups Metacrawler found searching" distance learning."

To read a message, click on that hyperlink to bring up a screen showing the full text. You will also see the name and e-mail address of the author, in case you want to follow up by e-mailing a comment or question. If you find that a number of relevant messages have been posted to one or more newsgroups, you may want to subscribe so you can receive any subsequent postings and join the discussion by posting your own messages. However, be aware that many newsgroups contain commercial postings as well as a wide range of personal opinions, so use good judgment to analyze and evaluate what you read.

Although these examples have focused on searches for "distance learning," you should try searches using other words or phrases to locate additional resources. For example, a search for "distance education" on the Web or in newsgroups will result in a different listing of hyperlinks. Remember that Web sites and newsgroups are constantly changing, so your results will probably look different from the results shown here—and any searches you conduct in the future are likely to return different results from those you conduct today.

A Distance Learning Sampler

To supplement your search efforts, you may want to take a few minutes to browse the following Web sites, just a small sample of the many distance learning opportunities available on the Internet. Some of these sites contain hyperlinks to other programs or additional sources of information that can be useful as you expand your search.

General Information

- Is distance learning right for you? Take this short online self-test from Waukesha County Technical College, WI—and find out. http://www.waukesha.tec.wi.us/pro.htm

- Tips for success: how to get the most from any distance learning opportunity, from the College of DuPage, IL. http://www.dupage.edu/excel.html

- Find and evaluate college-level distance learning courses using the Distance Learning Resource Network's listing of printed and Internet resources. http://www.fwl.org/edtech/CollegeDistanceEd.html

- Browse categorized listings of hyperlinks for distance learning programs, technology providers, and sources of information about distance learning theory and technique. http://www.online.uillinois.edu/ramage/disted.html

Academic Credit

- The National Universities Degree Consortium Web site offers hyperlinks to 14 accredited universities that cooperatively offer distance learning courses for undergraduate and graduate degrees as well as certificate programs. Members include Kansas State University and Colorado State University. http://www.sc.edu/deis/NUDC

- The West Suburban Post-Secondary Chicago consortium of colleges and universities provides online access to distance learning courses through members such as College of DuPage, Illinois State University, and North Central College. http://www.dupage.edu/wspsc/index.html

- At the Electronic University Network Web site, students can browse the virtual campuses and courses of several colleges that offer online courses. http://www.wcc-eun.com/wln/campus/eun/index.html

- CASO's Internet University site contains a comprehensive listing of distance learning courses and providers with brief descriptions plus hyperlinks to more detailed data. http://www.caso.com/iu

- University of Minnesota offers undergraduate degrees using a variety of distance learning techniques, including Internet-based instruction. http://www.cee.umn.edu/dis/

- Ohio University Independent Study allows students to earn credit toward undergraduate degrees using various distance learning techniques, including e-mail. http://www.cats.ohiou.edu/~indstu/index.htm

- University of Phoenix offers numerous undergraduate and graduate courses (and continuing education courses); cyberstudents can earn a bachelor's or master's degree entirely through online study. http://www.uophx.edu/

Career Development

- Certificate programs in telecommunications are available through distance learning programs on the Internet from the University College of the University of Denver; students can also earn undergraduate and graduate degrees in a number of disciplines. http://www.du.edu/ucol/tele/teleidx.html

- The Continuing Professional Education program at University of Phoenix offers range of courses for enhancing professional proficiency. Try a free online orientation course to preview the learning method before registering. http://www.uophx.edu/cpeinet/

- The Indiana University School of Continuing Studies offers online certificate programs, credit and noncredit courses in labor studies, workforce development, and other management subjects. http://www.extend.indiana.edu/gs/cs.htm

- Professional certificates in accounting, business, and management are offered through the Internet by Champlain College Online in Vermont; associate and bachelor's degrees are also available. http://www.champlain.edu/OLDE/index.html

Personal Enrichment

- LearnItOnline from ZDNet (Ziff-Davis, publisher of tech magazines) offers online learning to help users get the most from programs such as Web browsers, word processing, and graphics software. http://www.learnitonline.com/

- Syracuse Continuing Education Online offers a variety of non-credit courses, including fiction writing, critical thinking, communication, psychology, and programming. http://www.suce.syr.edu/online/

- Practice reading and writing Italian online at the CyberItalian Web site; conduct a search of Yahoo! to locate other language courses on the Internet. http://cyberitalian.com/html/language.htm

- Composers in Electronic Residents, a Web site provided by York University, allows music students and teachers who use MIDI technology to interact with professional composers in an online environment. http://www.edu.yorku.ca/CIERmain.html

- The WhaleNet educational Web site, from Wheelock College in Boston, has everything you wanted to know about whales (and marine life)—and more. http://whale.wheelock.edu/

- Take an online poetry course from Clark College, Washington, including cyberchat sessions and hyperlinks to online poets around the United States. http://clark.edu/instruct/human/english/poetry/poetry.htm

10 Questions to Ask Before You Register

No matter what you want to achieve by taking a distance learning course, you should ask pointed questions before making any commitments. A little advance checking will help you determine the potential benefits and value of each course under consideration. Just as important, these questions will help you recognize potential problems, eliminate inappropriate courses, and narrow your options to identify the courses most suited to your particular needs and situation.

1. Who is offering the course?

Find out about the institution, company, or organization offering the course. If the sponsor appears to be an educational institution, is it a real college or university (or a legitimate affiliate)? Names can be deceiving: what sounds like a prestigious university may actually be a front for a rip-off, so do some checking. Similarly, if a company or professional organization is sponsoring the course, you will want to investigate the sponsor's reputation and background before you sign a contract or send money.

The address of the Web site can often provide some clues (*.com* indicates a for-profit site, while *.edu* indicates an educational site). Also look for contact information such as the sponsor or institution's address, phone and fax numbers, affiliations, and other details.

2. Is the course part of an accredited program?

Accreditation is a critical issue for students seeking to earn a recognized degree. If a distance learning course is part of an unaccredited program, you may not be able to transfer the credits to an institution with an accredited program. If you are interested in pursing a degree entirely by distance learning and then continuing to study for even higher degrees, you should be sure that your diploma and coursework will be recognized by other institutions and by potential employers.

Legitimate educational institutions can provide solid information about their accreditation and refer you to the accrediting body for more details. Be especially careful about checking the accreditation of for-profit sponsors—and check on the accrediting body, as well. Accreditation is a complex topic, so you may want to talk with an administrator at a nearby college or university as an initial step.

3. What is the time commitment?

This is actually a two-part question. First, find out about the time requirements for an individual course. How often students must "meet" for Cyberspace discussions (if ever)? How many meetings are required over the entire course? How much time is allowed for submitting assignments? How long you can expect the entire course to last? Must you log on a certain number of times or devote a given amount of time to coursework in order to obtain credit? For example, the Professional Real Estate Education Online program takes online attendance to ensure that students put in the required number of hours and complete the appropriate coursework to receive a certificate of completion.

Second, if you are planning to take distance learning courses to earn a degree, you will want to ask how many months or years students typically need to complete all their courses and qualify for graduation. In most cases, all courses are <u>not</u> offered all year-round, which can slow you down if you are trying to earn a degree more quickly. On the other hand, some institutions schedule courses more frequently, to accommodate students who are in a hurry. In addition, some institutions have regulations regarding the length of time a student can take to complete a degree, so check before you enroll.

4. What is the cost?

Ask about the tuition per course or per credit as well as any additional charges, such as registration or administration fees. Also ask about payment methods and schedules; nearly every school allows payment by major credit card, and some will accept payments in installments.

If textbooks or other learning materials must be purchased, take these into consideration when calculating the total cost of any distance learning course. Finally, consider the cost of dialing into the Internet to participate in the course.

5. What is the content?

Is the course merely an introduction to a topic—or is it an in-depth examination? Is the focus primarily on theory or will you also learn tips for practical application? Is the course covering the latest advances in the field? To answer these questions, you may have to go beyond the course description shown on the screen or in the catalog.

In some cases, you will have to contact the institution or sponsoring organization to get more details about the exact content of a particular course. Then ask yourself whether you are really interested in the course content—and whether the coverage will help you meet your goals.

6. What are the teacher's credentials?

Although some of what you learn in an online course will come from the text—and some from the comments and suggestions of other students—you will also want to look at your teacher's qualifications. How does the teacher's educational and/or work background fit with the course content? Has the teacher had much hands-on experience in applying what is being taught? How long has the teacher been teaching this or similar courses?

Many distance learning programs invite prospective students to read brief biographies of their faculty members. Before you sign up for a course, browse the Web site to read about the teachers so you can make an informed decision.

7. What are the entrance requirements or prerequisites?

As with traditional college or training programs, many distance learning programs impose entrance requirements or prerequisites. For example, some online master's or doctoral programs are open only to students with extensive work experience, just as some professional courses on the Internet are open only to those who have attained a particular standing or seniority in the industry.

A number of courses prevent students from enrolling in advanced courses unless they have taken lower-level courses as prerequisites. This is the case in many high-tech courses, where a basic knowledge of a particular programming language is generally required for admission. As a result, you should check on any requirements so you can plan to take courses in the appropriate order and at the appropriate point in your career.

8. How is the course conducted?

As discussed earlier, distance learning can take many forms. Before you sign up, you will want to take time to find out how your course will be conducted. Internet-based courses are often presented via a combination of e-mail, chat, electronic slide shows, and audio- or video-enhanced materials—in addition to a printed text. Some online courses may require a non-Internet component as well (such as teleconferencing).

A few schools allow students to try a sample class or course in advance; for example, Champlain College Online offers a sample course on Vermont history. Students simply sign up (**http://www.champlain.edu/**) and wait for e-mail instructions that explain how to log onto the system to access course materials.

As you investigate the way the course is conducted, also consider the communication between teachers and students. Are you expected to work individually or as part of a team of students to complete one or more class projects? How much e-mail interaction can you expect with the teacher? With other students? The answers to these questions will help you gauge whether a course fits your individual learning style and personal preferences.

9. What equipment is required?

At the very least, distance learning courses on the Internet require access to a properly-configured personal computer with modem, Web browsing software, and a dial-up connection to the Internet. Individual courses may require additional software, such as a word processing program for writing reports or technical software for completing assignments.

You can usually learn about equipment requirements in advance by reading the course description or checking the school's Web site for more information. If all else fails, send an e-mail to the institution or sponsor to inquire about the necessary equipment.

10. What assistance is available—and when?

In distance learning, students bear most of the responsibility for successful learning. However, there will be times when you decide to seek assistance. You may want guidance about courses; you may want help entering the Web site for a scheduled class "chat" session; or you may have some other problem or question. Some colleges and universities offer online assistance through self-guided tutorials or access to experts via e-mail. At Rogers University, for example, students can obtain academic counseling and career counseling by surfing the online counseling center on the school's Web site.

Be prepared: before you take any class, find out how and when you can obtain help. Although you may be eager to fix a problem at 2 a.m. so you can download an assignment right away, you may not be able to get help at that hour. So play it safe: ask for a name or department to contact and get a telephone number as well as an e-mail address in case you have an urgent request. You may even want to make a request to experience the help system first-hand before you register.

Learning in Cyberspace

How does a cyberstudent actually participate in a distance learning course on the Internet? The answer depends on the format of the course—and the student's individual learning style.

In this section, you will follow along as Vicky, an undergraduate cyberstudent enrolled in the University of Phoenix's online program, participates in the first week of a five-week Organizational Behavior course. Because this course is conducted entirely via online messages, the instructor's role is particularly critical.

The Instructor's Role

Chad Lewis, the instructor for this Organizational Behavior course, has been teaching online since the early days of Internet-based education. Following the University of Phoenix model, Chad carefully plans his courses to provide a distinct structure to the learning experience.

Online courses at University of Phoenix start on Thursdays, with each course divided into five weeklong "workshops" covering related topics. By the time his cyberstudents dial into the school's computer system on the first Thursday of the course, Chad has already posted his initial lecture notes and assignments. He will continue to post new lecture notes and assignments every Thursday until the final week of the course.

Throughout the five weeks, Chad goes online several times each day to read student messages, respond to their comments, and help those who have questions about the coursework or the mechanics. His written syllabus lets students know exactly when their assignments are due; he also requires class "participation"—students must read their classmates' answers and reports, then post responses. By sticking to an established timetable and maintaining an online active presence, Chad adds structure to the learning process—the online equivalent of attendance in a regularly-scheduled class in a physical school facility.

In addition, Chad carries on a private e-mail correspondence with each student. (Students can also call or fax instructors with any questions or concerns.) By noon on Saturdays, Chad makes it a point to have all homework graded and returned to his students' private mailboxes. This feedback allows students to track their progress. "In an online environment, instructors can never give students too much feedback," he says. "Students need to know how they are doing and what is expected of them."

Getting Ready for Class

Before Vicky can attend online classes at the University of Phoenix, she must apply for admission; register for each course; receive confirmation of acceptance into the class; install special software for class communication; and order the course materials (in this case, a textbook, a book of supplementary readings, and a course curriculum). Students are expected to log onto the class meeting at least five out of seven days so they can read messages and post responses. Because the coursework is so intense, students are allowed to take only one five-week class at a time.

When Vicky launches the school's software and logs onto the system Thursday morning, she finds two messages from Chad, her instructor. One contains his biography, with the request that students upload their own biographies to the class meeting as soon as possible.

The second message presents the course syllabus, with the content and assignments for each of the five week-long workshops. From that message, Vicky learns that each week-long workshop will follow a particular schedule:

- Thursday: The instructor posts a new lecturette in the "class meeting" section of the online system.
- Saturday: After reading the corresponding text materials, students upload answers to questions posed in the lecturette.
- Sunday: Students prepare either a case analysis or a short report and upload it to the "cases and reports" section of the online system.
- Wednesday: Students write and submit a brief summary of the most meaningful learning experiences gained from that week's workshop, including an analysis of how they can apply the knowledge in their work life.

After the first week, Vicky will be sure to check her private e-mailbox every Saturday for graded homework returned (with comments) by the instructor. Once she downloads and prints the syllabus and the first week's lecturette, she is ready to participate in the first workshop.

Class Is In Session

With syllabus in hand, Vicky is ready for the first week of the course.

Thursday

When Vicky comes home from work on Thursday, she writes a one-page biography, adds a sentence about the prospects for her local baseball team, and logs on to upload this message to the class meeting. Already, five of the 12 students have posted their biographies. Todd is an engineer working in Cleveland; Amelia is a nurse who has just moved to San Diego; Curtis is interviewing for a new manufacturing job in Houston; Roberto is a systems analyst in Nashville; and Cindy is an assistant manager in a New Haven store.

Vicky notices that Roberto has also posted a message for Curtis, asking whether any students from their previous online class will be in the Organizational Behavior class. To break the ice, Vicky posts a message for Todd, introducing herself and asking whether he knows her cousin, who works in Cleveland. Then she logs off, reads the lecturette, and starts reading the first of the two chapters required for that week's workshop, which focuses on the nature and functions of management.

Late Thursday evening, Vicky logs on again and downloads the biographies of four more students. She also finds a message from Todd, who doesn't know her cousin but does share her interest in baseball. Vicky posts a brief message for Chad, the instructor, to ask about the textbooks he has written. Then she logs off, ending her first day in that week's workshop.

Friday

At dinnertime on Friday, Vicky goes online to download the biographies of the last two students. Three other students have posted messages commenting on Vicky's biography and asking a question or two about her background. Chad has posted a response to Vicky's question (as well as responses to two other students' comments or questions).

Later that evening, Vicky finishes reading the second chapter in the textbook and the two supplemental readings. Then she logs on to the class meeting and reads the messages from the students who have posted their answers to the instructor's questions.

Saturday

On Saturday morning, Vicky rereads the lecturette questions. Then she drafts her answers, logs onto the system, and uploads her work. Next, she reads through all the other students' answers—making notes as she reads—then types her response to each. She questions one student's defense of scientific management, but agrees with another that total quality management is a key competitive tool, based on her company's experience in the global marketplace.

Later that day, Vicky writes a first draft of her case analysis, citing sources in the text and the supplemental readings. If she wants to look for extra sources to supplement the text, she can tap into the search facilities of the University of Phoenix's Web-based library resource.

Sunday

By mid-day Sunday, Vicky is back at her computer, putting the finishing touches on her case analysis. She logs onto the system, uploads this assignment, and then reads all the new messages. This is the fourth day of the workshop, and she has read through nearly 100 messages posted in the class meeting.

Reading and responding to her classmates' messages takes time, but the process gives Vicky a more in-depth understanding of the concepts and their application to real-world situations. In fact, as she reads the comments posted by other students, Vicky begins to rethink her own answers.

Tuesday

Although she is too busy on Monday to log on to the class meeting, Vicky goes online early Tuesday morning to read more messages and to respond to her classmates' comments about her case analysis. Some agree with her ideas, citing their own reading and on-the-job experiences, while some argue for a slightly different approach. Chad has responded to some of the student comments, as well. Rather than immediately respond, Vicky prints the messages and logs off to read them more carefully. Then, before dinner, she goes online again to post her responses and read the next batch of messages posted by her classmates.

Wednesday

On Wednesday morning, Vicky checks the class meeting for any last-minute postings. Then she logs off and makes notes for her summary of the most meaningful learning experiences gained from the first weekly workshop. At the top of her list is her new awareness of the diversity of functions that any manager in any organization must perform. Next, she writes about the lively debate over scientific management—and her belief that creative, empowered employees are the essential ingredient in peak organizational performance. She ends her summary with a commitment to developing her own conceptual skills, since her attention to detail sometimes obscures the big picture.

Logging on before dinner to upload her summary, Vicky takes a few minutes to read what other students have posted. After typing a few messages in response, she logs off for the day. The second week-long workshop begins the next day, and Vicky wants to read ahead in preparation for the lecturette that will be posted in the class meeting on Thursday. It has been an intense week, but Vicky has enjoyed all the interaction with her classmates and she is looking forward to her instructor's comments on the homework assignment, which will be returned to her private e-mailbox on Saturday.

Class Is Over

During the fifth week of this Organizational Behavior course, Vicky downloads the final exam that Chad has posted in the class meeting. At this point, she has completed all the assignments and read through every online message posted by the instructor and the students. After she uploads the integrative report that serves as her final exam, she will wait a few days to find her final grades in her private e-mailbox—then the course will be over.

In addition to absorbing the basic concepts and thinking about their application to real work situations, Vicky has benefited from the insights offered by her diverse group of classmates. Although she has never actually seen Chad or any of her classmates, she feels as though she knows them through their online messages. Just as important, she was able to take the entire course without disrupting her ordinary work schedule, one of the key benefits of distance learning on the Internet.

Appendix I: Business-related Internet Addresses

As this booklet explains, once you're on the Internet, you can travel the globe. To get started, try the addresses that follow. They're grouped in various categories, but any one address may lead you to some totally unexpected sites. Experiment!

For information on our educational publications, in business, try the Prentice Hall Web site:
http://www.prenhall.com/phbusiness

	Site Name/Sponsor	Information	Address
Accounting	Rutgers University	Accounting education information	http://www.rutgers.edu/accounting/raw.html
	Edgar	Database of corporate information.	http://www.sec.gov/edgarhp.htm
	Edgar-Online	Up-to-the-minute corporate news.	http:/www.edgar-online.com/
	Professional Accounting Organizations	Springboard for locating many accounting organizations.	http://www.bus.orst.edu/
	American Accounting Association	Accounting education.	http://www.rutgers.edu/Accounting/raw/aaa/aaa.htm
	American Institute of Certified Public Accountants		http://www.rutgers.edu/Accounting/raw/aicpa/home.htm
	Institute of Management Accountants		http://panoptic.csustan.edu/ima/imafront.htm
	Accounting Companies/Organizations		http://www.library.ualberta.ca/library_html/subjects/accounting/links_accounting.htm
Businesses (Home pages)	IBM		http://www.ibm.com
	Charles Schwab & Co.		http://www.schwab.com
	GE Information Services		http://www.geis.com
	Texas Instruments		http://www.ti.com
	American Century Investments		http://www.americancentury.com
	Toyota		http://www.toyota.com
	Zenith Data Systems		http://www.zds.com
	3M Innovation Network		http://www.mmm.com
	Aetna		http://www.aetna.com
	American Stock Exchange		http://www.amex.com
	Ameritech		http://www.ameritech.com
	AT&T		http://www.att.com/
	Bell Atlantic		http://www.bell-atl.com
	Canon		http://www.usa.canon.com
	Chrysler		http://www.chryslercorp.com
	Compaq		http://www.compaq.com
	Federal Express		http://www.fedex.com/
	Ford		http://www.ford.com
	Hewlett-Packard		http://www.hp.com
	Kodak		http://www.kodak.com
	Eli Lilly & Co.		http://www.lilly.com
	Lotus		http://www.lotus.com
	MCI		http://www.mci.com
	Microsoft		http://www.microsoft.com
	Motorola		http://www.mot.com
	Novell		http://www.novell.com
	Raytheon		http://www.raytheon.com
	Siemens		http://www.siemens.com
	Sun Microsystems		http://www.sun.com
	Unisys		http://www.unisys.com
	UPS		http://www.ups.com
Business Law	Legal Information Institute		http://www.law.cornell.edu/supct.
	Supreme Court		http://supct.law.cornell.edu/
	PH BLAW		http://www.prenhall.com/phblaw
	Ray August - Professor of Business Law		http://www.wsu.edu:8080/~august

	ABA Lawlink	ABA legal research selected starting points	http://www.abanet.org/lawlink/home.html
	Law Resources on the Internet		http://www.rbvdnr.com/lawres.htm
	Academy of Legal Studies in Business		http://miavx1.acs.muohio.edu/%7Eherrondj/
Business Publications	Inc. Magazine		http://www.inc.com
	Dow Jones	Access to the publisher of The Wall Street Journal	http://bis.dowjones.com
	Electronic newsstand	A long list includes business publications.	http://www.enews.com
Business Statistics	SPSS	Statistical product and service solutions.	http://www.spss.com
	Statistics on the Web	Various statistical resources.	http://www.execpc.com/~helberg/statistics.html
	Basic Sources of Economic Statistics		http://www.princeton.edu/~econlib/basic.html
	A Guide to Statistical Computing Resourceson the Internet		http://asa.ugl.lib.umich.edu/chdocs/statistics/stat_guide_home.html
Finance/ Economics	Woodrow	Has a wide variety of financial information about banking, etc.; sponsored by Federal Reserve Bank of Minneapolis	http://woodrow.mpls.frb.fed.us
	Edgar	Database of corporate information.	http://www.sec.gov/edgarhp.htm
	Dun & Bradstreet Credit Information		http://www.dnb.com
	Money Magazine Personal Finance Center		http://www.pathfinder.com/money
	Corporate Finance Network		http://www.corpfinet.com
	Hoovers Online		http://www.hoovers.com
	The U.S. Tax Code Online		http://www.fourmilab.ch/ustax/ustax.html
	PC Quote		http://www.pcquote.com
	Investor Web		http://www.investorweb.com/
	MIT Stock Master		http://www.stockmaster.com
	Chicago Mercantile Exchange		http://www.cme.com/index.html
	The Syndicate		http://www.moneypages.com/syndicate/
	FinanceNet	Financial Management in Business	http://www.financenet.gov/
	Wall Street Journal Money & Investing Update		http://update.wsj.com/
General Reference	Webster's Dictionary		http://www.m-w.com/dictionary.htm
	List of American Universities		http://www.clas.ufl.edu/CLAS/american-universities.html
	AT&T Toll-Free Number Directory		http://att.net/dir800/
	CNN Financial Network Reference Desk		http:cnnfn.com/researchit/referencedesk/
	Listing of associations on the WWW		http://www.asaenet.org/Gateway/OnlineAssocSlist.html
	Better Business Bureau	Directory, national information.	http://www.bbb.org
	The List	List of 5,023 Internet service providers	http://thelist.iworld.com/
	Mondaq Business Briefing		http://www.mondaq.com
	Dun & Bradstreet	Data on millions of U.S. companies.	http://www.dnb.com
Government Resources	Library of Congress	A premier research library	http://lcweb.loc.gov/homepage/lchp.html
	National Technology Transfer Center	Connects private sector business with Federal lab system.	http://iridium.nttc.edu/nttc.html
	U.S. Patent and Trademark Office		http://www.uspto.gov
	Commerce Information Locator Service	Access to Department of Commerce databases.	http://www.doc.gov
	F.E.D. Resource Library		http://www.fed.org/library/index.html
	Central Intelligence Agency	Access to CIA World Factbook.	http://www.odci.gov
	Census Bureau	Social and economic indicators.	http://www.census.gov
Human Resources	HR Professional's Gateway to the Internet	Eric Wilson's home page, contains numerous HR-related Internet links.	http://www.wp.com/mike-shelley/
	AFL-CIO	Home page of the AFL-CIO, a labor federation to which most U.S. labor unions belong.	http://www.aflcio.org/
	American Compensation Association	Home page of the American Compensation Association, an organization of professionals engaged in the design, implementation, and management of employee compensation programs.	http://www.acaonline.org/
	Americans with Disabilities Act (ADA) Document Center	Provides numerous links to ADA resources, including sites regarding such specific disabilities as cancer, hearing impairment, and alcohol and drug-related illnesses.	http://janweb.icdi.wvu.edu/kinder/
	Benefits Link	Provides information on a wide variety of employee benefits plans.	http://www.benefitslink.com/index.shtml
	Career Mosaic	Contains a wealth of career and job information, including a large database of current job opportunities.	http://www.careermosaic.com/
	HR Magazine	Articles form HR Magazine, published monthly by the Society for Human Resource Management.	http://www.shrm.org/docs/Hrmagazine.html
	Training Net	An information resource for those interested in training issues.	http://trainingnet.com/
	Thunderbird School of International Management	Provides access to outstanding sources of international business and HR information.	http://www.t-bird.edu/
Management	Institute of Management & Administration		http://www.ioma.com
	Academy of Management		http://www.aom.pace.edu
	Small Business Administration		http://www.sbaonline.sba.gov/

	U.S. Department of Commerce Information Service		http://www.doc.gov
	International Institute for Management Development	A focus on executive development from an international perspective.	http://www.imd.ch/
Marketing	U.S. Census Bureau	Has data on demographics from the U.S. census	http://www.census.gov
	American Demographics Magazine		http://www.marketingtools.com
	Nielsen Media Research	Nielsen contains perhaps the most authoritative study on Internet demographics.. The study follows the most reliable methodology for obtaining a random and representative population sample.	http://www.nielsen.com
	SRI - Stanford Research Institute	The Stanford Research Institute provides some of the best psychographic research on Web users. The site allows you to determine you own VALS and iVALS type.	http://future.sri.com
	Advertising Age	Madison Avenue's daily news and account changes for the industry's two news sources. Online access to new media and marketing coverage from Interactive Media & Marketing.	http://www.adage.com/
	Adweek Online	Site includes article archives from Adweek, Brandweek, and Mediaweek - and access to Adweek databases, such as Accounts I Review and Adweek's Client/Brand directory.	http://www.adweek.com/
	American Association of Advertising		http://www.commercepark.com/AAAA/
	Web Digest for Marketers		http://wdfm.com/
Operations Management	Operations Management Index		http://www.wbs.warwick.ac.uk/omindex/bib/
	Operations Research/Management Science	A focus on decision/risk analysis.	http://www.lumina.com/DA/
	Operations Research	Wide range of newsgroups, discussion groups, papers, and more.	http://www.rrz.uni-koeln.de/themen/or/
	Network Resources for Operations Research		http://mat.gsia.cmu.edu/resource.html
Org. Behavior	The Keirsey Temperament Sorter	Understand your personality and how it shapes your behavior	http://www.keirsey.com/cgi-bin/keirsey/newkts.cgi
	Entrepreneur Magazine	A wealth of information for aspiring entrepreneurs and small business managers.	http://www.entrepreneurmag.com/
	The Business Process Reengineering Online Learning Center	An excellent source for articles and reviews, book abstracts, mailing lists and forums, and reference lists and Web sites related to reengineering and business process reengineering teams.	http://www.prosci.com/index.htm
	Psychology Centre	Learn to distinguish between reinforcing and nonreinforcing consequences in complexorganizational situations.	http://server.bmod.athabascau.ca/html/prtut/reinpair.htm
Small Business Mgmt	Small Business Administration		http://www.sbaonline.sba.gov
	FranNet	General franchiser information.	http://www.frannet.com
	American Individual Magazine & Coffeehouse		http://aimc.com/aimc/
	Institute of Management and Administration	Links to hundreds of business sites.	http://www.ioma.com/index.html
	Franchise Handbook Online	Franchising opportunities.	http://www.franchise1.com/
	National Small Business Development Center	Small business and entrepreneurial opportunities.	http://www.smallbiz.suny.edu/
	Research Network		
	World M&A Network	Companies for sale, merger candidates.	http://www.worldm-anetwork.com/
	Resources for the Entrepreneur		http://www.DraperVC.com/Resources.html
Student Success	Tripod	Wide variety of educational and career resources for students, including online resume service and database	http://www.tripod.com
	JobTrak	Online resume and recruitment service; posts over 500 new job listings a day	http://www.jobtrak.com
	"Best Bets from the Net"	Lists the best sites for career hunting; maintained and created by two professors from the University of Michigan.	http://www.lib.umich.edu/
	Career Magazine	Online magazine that sponsors moderate career forums	http://www.careermag.com
	The Accounting.com Home Page	Source for employment opportunities in finance	http://www.accounting.com
	Job Hunter		http://www.collegegrad.com/
	Occupational Outlook Handbook		http://stats.bls.gov:80/ocohome.htm
	America's Job Bank	List of all the government jobs available in U.S. State Employment Offices	http://www.ajb.dni.us/

Appendix II
Glossary

Background — This refers to an image or color that is present in the background of a viewed Web document. Complex images are becoming very popular as backgrounds but require a great deal more time to download. The color of default background can be set for most Web browsers.

Bookmark — This refers to a list of URLs saved within a browser. The user can edit and modify the bookmark list to add and delete URLs as the user's interests change. Bookmark is a term used by Netscape to refer to the user's list of URLs; Hotlist is used by Mosaic for the same purpose. (See *Hotlist*, *Mosaic*, and *URL*.)

Browser — A browser is a software program that runs on a personal computer and provides a graphical user interface (GUI) to the Web. The two most popular browsers are Netscape Navigator (or Communicator) and Microsoft Internet Explorer.

Bulletin Board Service — This is an electronic bulletin board. It is sometimes referred to as a BBS. Information on a BBS is posted to a computer where people can access, read, and comment on it. A BBS may or may not be connected to the Internet. Some are accessible by modem dial-in only.

Chat room — This is a site that allows for real-time person-to-person interactions.

Clickable image (Clickable map) — This refers to an interface used in Web documents that allow the user to click, or select, different areas of an image and receive different responses. Clickable images are becoming a popular way to offer a user many different selections within a common visual format.

Client — This is a software program used to view information from remote computers. Clients function in a Client-Server information exchange model. This term may also be loosely applied to the computer that is used to request information from the server. (See *Server*.)

Compressed file — This refers to a file or document that has been compacted to save memory space so that it can be easily and quickly transferred through the Internet.

Cyberspace — Cyberspace is used to describe the environment which users enter into on the Net.

Download — This is the process of transferring a file, document, or program from a remote computer to a local computer. (See *Upload*.)

Domain Name — Domain names are used to address sites on the Internet. The top-level domain names are com, edu, gov, net, and org. Second level domain names usually correspond to familiar trademarks like Coca-Cola, McDonalds, Pepsi, etc.

E-mail This is the short name for electronic mail. E-mail is sent electronically from one person-to another. Some companies have e-mail systems that are not part of the Internet. E-mail can be sent to one person or to many different people. (I sometimes refer to this as Junk E-mail.)

Ethernet Ethernet refers to the most popular transport technology standard used in local area networks (LANs).

FAQ Frequently Asked Questions (FAQs) often appear as a link on the home pages of different sites.

Frame Relay Frame Relay refers to the most popular transport technology standard used in wide area networks (WANs).

Forms This refers to an interface element used within Web documents to allow the user to send information back to a Web server. With a forms interface, the user is requested to type responses within entry windows to be returned to the server for processing. Forms rely on a server computer to process the submittals. They are becoming more common as browser and server software improve.

GUI Is an acronym for Graphical User Interface. It is a combination of the appearance and the method of interacting with a computer. A GUI requires the use of a mouse to select commands on an icon-based monitor screen. Macintosh and Windows operating systems are examples of typical GUIs.

Helper This is software that is used to help a browser view information formats that it couldn't normally view.

Home Page A Home Page is first page that you see when you visit a site (e.g., www.honda.com). Sites often have many different home pages if they host many different users. In this case you must know the subdirectory where the users home page is located (e.g., wwwsb.ccsu.ctstateu.edu/faculty/frost/460).

Host A host is a computer on the Web. The term is used interchangeably with site.

HTML An abbreviation for HyperText Markup Language, the common language used to write documents that appear on the World Wide Web.

HTTP An abbreviation for HyperText Transport Protocol, the common protocol used to communicate between World Wide Web servers.

Hyperlink Hyperlinks are text or graphics that link to other pages on the Web.

Hypertext This refers to text elements within a document that have an embedded connection to another item. Web documents use hypertext links to access documents, images, sounds, and video files from the Internet. The term hyperlink is a general term that applies to elements on Web pages other than text.

Internet The Internet is the global inter-network of computers. Major uses of the Internet include e-mail and Web browsing.

Intranet Intranets employ Internet technology to form home pages that are internal to a company. The Intranet serves as an easily accessible repository for corporate information—anything from strategic targets to health plans. Intranets capitalize on the fact that most organizations distribute far more information internally than they do to the outside world.

ISP Internet Service Providers are companies that sell access to the Internet.

Java This is an object-oriented programming language developed by *Sun Microsystems.*

JavaScript This is a scripting language developed by Netscape in cooperation with *Sun Microsystems* to add functionality to the basic Web page. It is not as powerful as Java and works primarily from the client side.

LAN A Local Area Network connects computers in an organization allowing them to communicate and share resources such as printers and Internet connections.

Link See hyperlink

Modem A modem is a device that translates computer signals into sound waves and back again to allow two computers to communicate over a phone line. Its name comes from the fact that it modulates computer signals to sound and demodulates sound back to computer signals. Today's fastest modems receive data at about 50,000 characters per second.

Mosaic This is the name of the browser that was created at the National Center for Supercomputing Applications. It was the first Web browser to have a consistent interface for the Macintosh, Windows, and UNIX environments. The success of this browser is responsible for the expansion of the Web.

Net Net is short for Internet.

Newsgroup This the name for the discussion groups that can be on the Usenet. Not all news groups are accessible through the Internet. Some are accessible only through a modem connection. (See Usenet.)

Open text search An open text search looks for word matches when given a search string.

Plug-in This is a resource that is added to Netscape to extend its basic function.

QuickTime This is a format used by Apple Computer to make, view, edit, and send digital audio and video.

Server This is a software program used to provide, or serve, information to remote computers. Servers function in a Client-Server information exchange model. This term may also be loosely applied to the computer that is used to serve the information. (See *Client.*)

Site A site is a computer on the Internet. Site is also used to refer to a home page (e.g., "great Web site").

Subject tree search A subject tree search requires that the user navigate by progressively more specific subjects until they find the information for which they are looking.

T1 A T1 line is a high-speed telecommunications line used by larger organizations. T1 lines have 24 64 Kbps channels. A fractional T1 line uses only some of the available channels.

Table This refers to a specific formatting element found in HTML pages. Tables are used on HTML documents to visually organize information.

Telnet This is the process of remotely connecting and using a computer at a distant location.

Upload This is the process of moving or transferring a document, file, or program from one computer to another computer.

URL This is an abbreviation for Universal Resource Locator. In its basic sense it is an address used by people on the Internet to locate documents. URLs have a common format that describes the protocol for information transfer, the host computer address, the path to the desired file, and the name of the file requested.

Usenet This is a world-wide system of discussion groups, also called newsgroups. There are many thousands of newsgroups, but only a percentage of these are accessible from the Internet.

WAN Wide Area Networks (WANs) connect different divisions of an organization that are located across the city, across the country, or across the world from one another.

Web (WWW) The World Wide Web (WWW) defines a standard for navigating between computers on the Internet using hyperlinks.